Once, when a child, I ⟨...⟩ book. The giver had ⟨...⟩ 'The Fear of the Lor⟨...⟩

It seemed at the ⟨...⟩ unfriendly, as though I was being ⟨...⟩ for my foolishness. I was a sensitive child.

A few days ago I came across this book whilst sorting out a box of old possessions, and again I was struck by the sternness of the message. The difference now, however, is that I understand the importance of those words, since the fear of the Lord had indeed changed my life.

What is wisdom? The dictionary defines it as 'knowledge of what is true and right, coupled with just judgement as to action'.

It is something we all long for especially as the journey through life brings us up against problems which leave us feeling confused and inadequate.

The Bible is without doubt the greatest source of wisdom we have. Melvin Tinker has used some of the great passages from Proverbs, Psalms, Ecclesiastes and the Epistles, to expand our thoughts and present to us in a friendly and readable way the fundamentals of wisdom we need today in our everyday lives, and how to apply them through God's Word.

Wendy Craig
well-known Christian actress

Starting with the coronation gift to the sovereign of the Bible as 'the most valuable thing that this world affords', Melvin Tinker demonstrates the sheer wisdom of select Bible passages as they address contemporary concerns – euthanasia, self-worth, marriage, family etc. He shows convincingly that living biblically in a complex world is not old-fashioned: it is wisdom.

Michael Green
Archbishop of Canterbury's
advisor on Evangelism

Wisdom to live by

Living Biblically in a complex world

Melvin Tinker

Christian Focus

ISBN 1 85792 502 5

Published in 1998
by Christian Focus Publications
Geanies House, Fearn, Ross-shire,
IV20 1TW, Great Britain

Cover design by Owen Daily

Contents

For Heather.
Proverbs 31:10.

Preface

'We present you with this Book, the most valuable thing that this world affords. Here is wisdom; this is the royal law; these are the lively oracles of God.' With these words in the coronation service the Moderator of the General Assembly of the Church of Scotland handed to the newly crowned Queen Elizabeth a copy of the Bible.

Is this excessive rhetoric or sober realism?

The cynic might well argue for the former, dismissing such words as a pious hope which is no more than a sentimental hangover from a previous age. Today we are in a 'post modern' situation where such certainty regarding the true value of a text (let alone an ancient text such as the Bible) cannot be attained. Everything is relative, what 'works' or creates an emotional, existential impact is the only measure we have of a book's value.

But why should truth and pragmatism, abiding relevance and emotive import be set in opposition to each other? If God is the God of truth, the Creator of the Universe, the one who 'knows the end from the beginning', then surely we should expect that his revealed truth should work for the best, should be timeless in its relevance and move us at the deepest level of our being?

Millions of people, from different ages and cultures throughout the world, have found that this has proved to be the case. They have discovered that in reading the Bible a miracle occurs – God speaks. He speaks with sober realism into people's lives, truths which resonate with the reality of the world as it is, as well as touching those chords in the human heart which aspire for something better, a longing for a world as it should be. So we have the great eighteenth-century American preacher and theologian, Jonathan Edwards, writing about his experience in reading the Bible in this way:

> 'Oftentimes in reading it, every word seemed to touch my heart. I felt a harmony between something in my heart, and those sweet and powerful words. I seemed often to see so much light exhibited in every sentence, and such refreshing food communicated, that I could not get along in reading; often dwelling long on one sentence, to see the wonders contained in it; yet almost every sentence seemed to be full of wonders.'[1]

As the Moderator rightly said of the Bible to Queen Elizabeth, 'Here is wisdom.'

We live in a world which has largely abandoned the notion of wisdom, eschewing the cumulative insights of previous generations in the belief that 'the latest is the greatest'. This is both

---

1. Jonathan Edwards, *Personal Narrative*, Selections, 65, eds C.H. Faust and T. Johnson (New York: Hill and Wang, 1935).

dangerous and foolish, as experience eventually confirms.

The Bible, however, insists on the supreme value of wisdom, especially heavenly wisdom (e.g. Jas. 1:5). Its function is to keep us in touch with reality, to help us steer a steady course through this world as chartered by God's own revelation and enabled by God's own Spirit – the Spirit of wisdom.

In this book several contemporary topics are considered from the biblical standpoint of wisdom, wisdom as found in both the Old and New Testaments. It is hoped that the reader will be excited in seeing how relevant the Bible, perhaps to him or her a surprising source, can be in dealing with issues which vex many today. It is also hoped that this will lead to a renewed confidence in the sufficiency of Scripture as well as the willingness to be challenged to think and act Christianly as 'salt and light' in the world God has placed us.

It has often been remarked upon that preachers are like magpies, snatching good things from a variety of places. Where possible I have attempted to note the original references to quotations. Some are included from memory, other influences are more unconscious. All the faults are my own.

I would like to express my appreciation to the staff of St. John's Newland, for all the wisdom they have shared with me in their teaching and practical support. Also for the love and fellowship of the church family at St. John's in which so many of these chapters began life in the context of preaching. Thanks, too, is in order to Shirley Godbold, who in her own time took the effort to read through and correct the manuscript. Her tireless kindness and help never ceases to amaze me and for this I am most grateful.

Last, but not least, I want to acknowledge my deepest gratitude to my wife, Heather, for all the wisdom she has shown to me over the years which has always been so lovingly practical and timely. This book is dedicated to her.

Melvin Tinker,
St. John's, Newland,
Hull.
1999.
Soli Deo Gloria.

1

What's it all about ?
Wisdom for life
Ecclesiastes

Ecclesiastes 12

[1]Remember your Creator
    in the days of your youth,
before the days of trouble come
    and the years approach when you will say,
    'I find no pleasure in them' –
[2]before the sun and the light
    and the moon and the stars grow dark,
    and the clouds return after the rain;
[3]when the keepers of the house tremble,
    and the strong men stoop,
when the grinders cease because they are few,
    and those looking through the windows grow dim;
[4]when the doors to the street are closed
    and the sound of grinding fades;
when men rise up at the sound of birds,
    but all their songs grow faint;
[5]when men are afraid of heights
    and of dangers in the streets;
when the almond tree blossoms
    and the grasshopper drags himself along
    and desire no longer is stirred.
Then man goes to his eternal home
    and mourners go about the streets.

⁶Remember him – before the silver cord is severed,
　　or the golden bowl is broken;
before the pitcher is shattered at the spring,
　　or the wheel broken at the well,
⁷and the dust returns to the ground it came from,
　　and the spirit returns to God who gave it.
⁸'Meaningless! Meaningless!' says the Teacher.
　　'Everything is meaningless!'

⁹Not only was the Teacher wise, but also he imparted knowledge to the people. He pondered and searched out and set in order many proverbs. ¹⁰The Teacher searched to find just the right words, and what he wrote was upright and true.

¹¹The words of the wise are like goads, their collected sayings like firmly embedded nails – given by one Shepherd. ¹²Be warned, my son, of anything in addition to them.

Of making many books there is no end, and much study wearies the body.

¹³Now all has been heard;
　　here is the conclusion of the matter:
Fear God and keep his commandments,
　　for this is the whole duty of man.
¹⁴For God will bring every deed into judgment,
　　including every hidden thing,
　　whether it is good or evil.

There is a rather amusing story of the man who, having a jealous streak, began to doubt whether his wife was being faithful to him. So, he devised a plan that one day he would pretend to go off to work but would wait nearby and then rush into the third floor flat where he and his spouse lived, to confirm his worst suspicions. That is precisely what he did. Having kissed his wife good-bye and supposedly setting off for work, he waited around the corner, counted to a hundred, then dashed back into the block of flats, raced upstairs, burst into the room, and saw his wife looking out of the window. Smelling cigarette smoke, he thought the worst, glanced out of the window only to see a man climbing into a white sports car clutching a bunch of flowers. In a fit of rage, he dashed back into the kitchen, picked up the fridge, ran back to the window and hurled it on the man below. In the event, it proved too much for his old heart, and that was the end for him.

Imagine a change of scene. St. Peter is at the gates of heaven when the jealous husband turns up. 'What happened to you?' asks Peter. 'Well, I have always had this insane jealousy,' confessed the man. 'Rather foolishly suspecting my wife of being unfaithful, I picked up a fridge to throw at the fellow and, well, here I am.' 'Alright' said Peter, 'just wait over there.' Next came a man with a big bandage wrapped around his head, limping on crutches – battered and bruised. 'What happened to you?' enquired Peter. 'You will not believe this,' replied the man, 'it was the funniest thing. There I was on the way to work and I thought it would be nice to surprise my wife by nipping into the corner shop to buy some flowers. But as I was getting into my car, I heard this whistling sound, only to look up and see a gigantic refrigerator hurtling towards me.' 'Oh,' said Peter, 'well, you just wait over there.'

Then appeared another fellow, looking rather sheepish. 'And what's your story?' asked Peter. 'Well,' said the man, 'I was hiding in this fridge...!'

What is the moral of that story? You can never be too sure how things will turn out. The writer of Ecclesiastes would entirely agree. When it comes to 'life under the sun', while it may be the case that some things are monotonously predictable – as he says in 1:4: 'Generations come and generations go, but the earth remains for ever. The sun rises and the sun sets, and hurries back to where it rises.' Other vicissitudes in life are far less certain and have an arbitrary, almost whimsical, quality to them. Just when you seem to have worked long and hard to enjoy that little nest egg you have put aside, for no apparent reason it is all taken away: 'I have seen another evil under the sun, and it weighs heavily on men; God gives a man wealth, possessions and honour, so that he lacks nothing his heart desires, but God does not enable him to enjoy them, and a stranger enjoys them instead' (6:1). We have to admit, there are times when life does seem to be little more than a 'tale told by an idiot full of sound and fury' making very little sense.

A God-centred world view

But we are not to make the mistake of thinking that our writer is an atheist. He is clearly a believer in the one true God and it is this belief that there is a God who is there and who has spoken which provides the key to believing that, in spite of all its absurdity, life on the whole has direction and purpose. We can believe that the truth is out there because God is out there and we can know him. Indeed, it is in being in a right relationship with him that life takes on lasting significance – hence the conclusion at the end of the book in 12:13: 'Now all has been heard; here is the conclusion of the matter: Fear God and keep his command-ments, for this is the whole duty of man.'

Who is this writer? In 1:1 he is described as the 'Teacher, son of David'. The word for teacher is Qoheleth and means 'sage' or even 'philosopher'. A philosopher has been defined as someone who takes that which every-one can understand and turns it into that which no one can understand! But not this man. As we shall see, his observations are very astute and resonate with our own experience. He is not some dewy-eyed, armchair idealist who describes the world as he would like it to be, nor some hard-nosed cynic who cannot stand the world as it is, but a wide-eyed realist. The believer in the covenant God who speaks is the only one who can look life squarely in the face and say I understand why things are as they are, and why I am as I am, for God has given me sufficient explanations in his book, the Bible, and it makes sense.

You know it makes sense

Let me ask: do you want to know why deep down you feel you are important when everything around you tells you you are not, that you are just another insignificant speck of human stardust in an impersonal cosmos? Do you want to solve the paradox that the more you have the more you want and the less satisfied you seem to be? More than that, do you want to know the God for whom you were made and who can be your consummate joy and delight? If the answer is yes, however tentative, then listen to the philosopher.

1. Asking the right questions

First of all, the philosopher calls us to consider a realistic question: 'What does man gain from all his labour at which he toils under the sun?' (1:3) – literally, what profit is there to life? Can we ever be sure of attain-ing success in this life and being satisfied with it? If so, how? If not, what is the point of living?

Secondly, the philosopher calls us to take a realistic look at life. One of the main literary features of this book is its repetition of the key word translated 'meaningless' or 'vanity'. It appears over thirty-eight times. It is the philosopher's premise at the beginning in 1:2: 'Meaningless! Meaningless!' says the Teacher, 'Utterly meaningless! Everything is meaningless.' It is also his summary at the end of the book in 12:8. But what is he saying? Is it that nothing makes sense? That life at its heart is futile? Like the claim of the existentialist Jean Paul Sartre who says 'We are all of us eating and drinking to preserve our precious existence and there is nothing, no reason for existing.'

Is that it? It certainly sounds that way. But that would be to totally misunderstand the profound point the philosopher is making. The word translated 'meaningless' (*hebhel*) literally means 'breath' or 'vapour'. Someone has suggested that it might be translated 'bubbles'. That is, most of what we experience is transitory, here today and gone tomorrow, insubstantial, like chasing after the mist or trying to hold down a shadow. That is what life *feels* like 'under the sun'.

According to the Bible, this experience of dissatisfaction is but one piece of the evidence that we live in what is called a fallen world. It is morally and spiritually fractured, so life is like looking into a broken mirror, things appear distorted. And indeed they are, because we are out of sorts with our Maker.

We stand under his judgment, as does the whole of creation. We live east of Eden, restless, rootless, seeking a lasting home but finding none. As such we instinctively feel that things are not as they should be. We are reminded that this world is not our home but that we are made for something more, someone more, our Creator. The trouble is we have an ambivalent attitude towards him.

On the one hand we long for God and on the other hand we run from him. Accordingly, instead of seeking him out to find lasting meaning, we turn to other things instead to try and satisfy that deep, spiritual thirst inside, only to discover it is like drinking salt water; they are meaningless – *hebhel* – insubstantial. We can never find success in these things under the sun because we were never *meant* to find lasting profit in *them* but only in God.

So, some people turn to pleasure. The philosopher himself has gone down the road of the hedonist and this is what he observes:

'I thought in my heart, "Come now, I will test you with pleasure to find out what is good." But that also proved to be meaningless. "Laughter," I said, "is foolish. And what does pleasure accomplish?" I tried cheering myself with wine, and embracing folly – my mind still guiding me with wisdom. I wanted to see what was worth-while for men to do under heaven during the few days of their lives' (2:1-3).

We might think of the great comedian Peter Sellers. He pursued laughter in a big way, together with women, drink and drugs which eventually killed him. But this is what his friend, Spike Milligan, had to say of him towards the end of what was a completely selfish and tormented life: 'To try to know him [Peter Sellers] was like going to a desert island. He's that lonely. He's desperate to be happy, successful, wanted, happily married. He's desperate not to destroy his past. It's all desperation. He *is* desperation.' Isn't that a sad assessment by a friend? He was trying to answer the philosopher's question about the bottom line in life and sought it in pleasure and failed.

For others, it is fame that is thought to be the answer. The philosopher has tried that route too:

'Better a poor but wise youth than an old but foolish king who no longer knows how to take warning. The youth may have come from prison to the kingship, or he may have been born in poverty within his kingdom. I saw that all who lived and walked under the sun followed the youth, the king's successor. There was no end to all the people who were before them. But those who came later were not pleased with the successor. This too is meaningless, a chasing after the wind' (4:13-16).

Here is a rags to riches story – the progression from pauper to King. Advancement in our career, perhaps this will be lasting? The philosopher says no. Others would agree. Take the pop star

Madonna. She arrived in New York City with $35 in her pocket. Within a matter of a few years she was a multi-millionaire, with her hit single *Material Girl* epitomising the spirit of the eighties. Now she admits that she was driven and here is the reason she gives: 'When my mother died, all of a sudden I was going to become the best student, get the best grades; I was going to become the best singer, the best dancer, the most famous singer in the world. Everybody was going to love me. But,' she adds, 'I am a very tormented person. I want to be happy.'[1] She is like so many people today, lost in their own self-made image – demandingly using, pushing, shoving, yet beneath it all left feeling empty – meaningless.

Perhaps wealth is the key? 'Whoever loves money never has money enough; whoever loves wealth is never satisfied with his income. This too is meaningless' (5:10).

Once, the reporter Alan Wicker visited the home of Paul Getty, then the richest man on earth. At one point in the TV interview, Alan Wicker turned to the multi-millionaire and said, 'Mr. Getty, you seem to have everything. You have a paradise island, beautiful women, great works of art, yachts, everything it seems. Is there anything you don't have but would like?' Getty's response

---

1. Jock McGregor, 'Madonna: Icon of Postmodernity', L'Abri Lecture No 9.

was as quick as a flash. He replied, 'You can always want a little more.' And he probably hadn't even read Ecclesiastes! What is our culture shouting at us with its easy credit, mammoth lottery hand-outs? But that wealth *is* the way to lasting happiness. No, this, too, is chasing after the wind.

Others would go down the more noble path and say that the pursuit of wisdom itself, and academic education, is the surest road to attaining a long-lasting goal. Maybe science is the way ahead for bringing in Utopia to our planet? 'I undertook great projects: I built houses for myself and planted vineyards. I made gardens and parks and planted all kinds of fruit trees in them. I made reservoirs to water groves of flourishing trees' (2:4-6).

President John F. Kennedy once said that most of the problems on this planet have been caused by man and most of the problems can be solved by man through science. I don't find such optimism around today. The mood is more apocalyptic than utopian. Since then we have had Chernobyl, moral bewilderment regarding cloning, ecological imbalance caused by industrialisation. This is not to say that a wise use of science will not mitigate some of these effects, but it is far from certain that this is where the final answer lies.

22

2. Is there life before death?

But whatever achievements we have attained, we all have to face the great leveller, death, which does cast a dark question mark against the ultimate point of life. The comedian Woody Allen once put it like this:

> 'All we are left with is alienation, loneliness and emptiness verging on madness. The fundamental thing behind all motivation and all activity is the constant struggle against annihilation and against death. It renders anyone's accomplishments meaningless. It is not only that he, the individual dies, or that man dies, but that you struggle to do a work of art that will last and then you realise that the universe itself is not going to exist after a period of time.'[2]

This is the man who said that he didn't want to achieve immortality through his works, he wanted to achieve it through not dying! The sentiments are remarkably similar to those of the philosopher:

> 'This is the evil in everything that happens under the sun: The same destiny overtakes all. The hearts of men, moreover, are full of evil and there is madness in their hearts while they live, and afterwards they join the dead. Anyone who is among the living has hope – even a live dog is better off than a dead lion!
>
> For the living know that they will die,
>   but the dead know nothing;

---

2. Woody Allen, in Esquire Magazine, May, 1977.

they have no further reward,
>   and even the memory of them is forgotten.
Their love, their hate
>   and their jealousy have long since vanished;
never again will they have a part
>   in anything that happens under the sun'

>   (9: 3-6).

This is a realistic view of life. Life is made up of the good, the bad and the ugly because we live in a world standing under God's curse. That is why there is sickness, wars, crime and death — that is why Christians too will be subject to these things like everyone else. But it is still a world ordered and ruled by the Creator, which brings us to the third point.

3. Your God is too small

The philosopher calls us to a realistic view of God. Quite frankly, many of our views of God are too man-centred and too small.

'I have seen the burden God has laid on men. He has made everything beautiful in its time. He has also set eternity in the hearts of men; yet they cannot fathom what God has done from beginning to end. I know that there is nothing better for men than to be happy and do good while they live. That everyone may eat and drink, and find satisfaction in all his toil – this is the gift of God. I know that everything God does will endure forever; nothing can be added to it and nothing taken from it. God does it, so that men will revere him' (3:10-14).

This is what the living God is like, the God who is the truth, the one who has made himself known by speaking into our world by his Word, the Scriptures, in a way which we can understand. He is the all-wise God – he has made everything beautiful in its time – just right. He is the all-personal God too, for he has put eternity in our hearts, that is, a deep knowledge that he is there and we are made for him, that we are more than genetic re-duplicating machines living just for the now, but people made in his image, made for a love relationship to last for all eternity. He is the all-giving God, so, yes it is good to be happy, to receive the gifts he gives, food, wine, friends, health – *but* not as ends in themselves, trying to make them bear a weight they were never intended to bear as purveyors of meaning. Instead, they are to be seen as gifts which will lead us with gratitude back to the Giver. This is the eternal God who knows no end; he is the opposite of meaninglessness and vanity; he is the endless fount of all true meaning and lasting value and it is as we come to know him, love him and revere him that we discover real purpose in life.

Do it now, says the philosopher, while you are young, before it is too late and other things crowd God out of your life:

'Remember your Creator
        in the days of your youth,
    before the days of trouble come

25

and the years approach when you will say, "I
find no pleasure in them" –
before the sun and the light
and the moon and the stars grow dark,
and the clouds return after the rain'

(12:1-2).

There is a sense of urgency about it all.

A life-changing experience

Let me relate the story of Jill, a social worker
student I met when I was chaplain at Keele
University. Jill travelled the road of the philosopher, indeed she read a degree in the subject.
Having been brought up to believe in God, she
rejected it to become an atheist. She suffered for
seven years with anorexia, ran away from home,
sexually experimented with men and became a
communist. Her life, she admitted, had
degenerated into a living hell. Then she met up
with some Christians and having encountered the
living God through his Son, Jesus Christ, went on
to write these words:

'It is difficult to believe that I am only a few weeks
old as a Christian, my life has been revolutionised in
many ways. Previously, I could not sing and was only
attracted to tragic melodies; now, I sing frequently
and gladly the praises of my Lord, being released from
pain. Previously, I could not pray and found it a
distasteful activity, now speech comes to me and
praying with others is mutually helpful. Previously, I

could not read the Bible and considered it an antiquated and absurd text; now I am drawn towards it, and the words and deeds of Jesus strike me immediately as the truth. Previously, I could not enter a church, and was suspicious of the ministers; now, I can be at home there, with an affinity with all believers. Ordinarily, I would have feared such a dramatic transformation, yet nothing has been more natural for me, and the effortlessness of it all points to God working through me. I did not "will" such changes, yet I did not feel "compelled", and whilst I have not "chosen" to be, feel and think differently, now that I have experienced these things, I would never choose for them to be otherwise. Had I understood what was possible, no doubt I would have sought the Lord more actively!'

You may not have exactly travelled down that path but life isn't making that much sense to you. You are only too aware that what the philosopher says is true, the aching void is there and you want to make contact with your Maker. The way we are all to do that is by coming personally to *the* great Teacher of Wisdom, the Lord Jesus Christ, who is the one Shepherd who died for us and lives so that we too might live.

2

Simply the Best, God's Wisdom in Proverbs

Proverbs 1:1-7

¹The proverbs of Solomon son of David, king of Israel:
²for attaining wisdom and discipline;
    for understanding words of insight;
³for acquiring a disciplined and prudent life,
    doing what is right and just and fair;
⁴for giving prudence to the simple,
    knowledge and discretion to the young –
⁵let the wise listen and add to their learning,
    and let the discerning get guidance –
⁶for understanding proverbs and parables,
    the sayings and riddles of the wise.

⁷The fear of the LORD is the beginning of knowledge,
    but fools despise wisdom and discipline.

Proverbs 3:13-20

¹³Blessed is the man who finds wisdom,
    the man who gains understanding,
¹⁴for she is more profitable than silver
    and yields better returns than gold.
¹⁵She is more precious than rubies;
    nothing you desire can compare with her.
¹⁶Long life is in her right hand;
    in her left hand are riches and honour.
¹⁷Her ways are pleasant ways,
    and all her paths are peace.
¹⁸She is a tree of life to those who embrace her;
    those who lay hold of her will be blessed.

¹⁹By wisdom the LORD laid the earth's foundations,
    by understanding he set the heavens in place;
²⁰by his knowledge the deeps were divided,
    and the clouds let drop the dew.

Cynthia didn't know it, but she had just confronted the woman reporters had nicknamed 'the nun from hell'. 'Do you want to take me on? Come on, I'm ready,' invited the tough 61-year-old nun with a black patch over one eye.

Cynthia, a prostitute and drug addict, took a second look at her steely faced opponent and decided she had met her match. She reluctantly agreed to obey the strict rules of the homeless shelter Sister Connie runs in the heart of Chicago's tough south side.

Sister Connie's shelter is not a place where homeless women are mollycoddled. The residents rise at 6.30 a.m. Mothers must clean both their children and rooms before breakfast. Classes in parenting and life skills are compulsory. So are daily twelve-step programmes for substance abusers. And if Sister Connie suspects residents are hiding drugs she is not above calling in the SWAT team.

It is a tough love but it actually works. Only 4% of the women who pass through Sister Connie's place ever end up back in the shelter system, by contrast with nearly 40% of those who pass through Chicago's public system where no such rules apply. Sister Connie's secret is that she attaches moral demands to the assistance she gives. The most common cause of homelessness, Sister Connie believes, is lack of personal responsibility. Her aim is to give it back.

Today Cynthia works as a restaurant cook, rents her own flat, and supports her own children.[1]

If you think about it, what that nun is doing is applying sanctified common sense. It is what the Bible calls – 'wisdom.' Instead of going with the flow of popular sociological thinking that people are simply helpless victims of an impersonal system, Sister Connie has acted on the biblical view that men and women are morally responsible agents made in God's image. That is wisdom – God's truth designed to enable God's people to live in God's world, God's way. It is simply the best.

There is one book in the Bible which gathers, orders and presents such wisdom in the form of pithy sayings, riddles and allegorical musings and that is the Book of Proverbs.

We are told right at the beginning of that book in 1:1 that here we have 'proverbs of Solomon, son of David, king of Israel'. In 1 Kings 4:29ff we are presented with Solomon as the wise man *par excellence*, whom we are informed uttered 3,000 proverbs:

> 'God gave Solomon wisdom and very great insight, and a breadth of understanding as measureless as the sand on the seashore. Solo-mon's wisdom was greater than the wisdom of all the men of the East, and greater than all the wisdom of Egypt.... He spoke three thousand proverbs and his songs numbered a thousand and five.'

---

1. Charles Colson's *Burden of Truth*, Tyndale, 1997, p.17.

This does not necessarily mean that he devised all of those proverbs himself. There is every reason to believe that some were gleaned from other people (it has long been recognised for example, that the group of sayings in 22:12 is very similar to an Egyptian writing, *The Instruction of Amenemope*). Nonetheless, here we have the Holy Spirit using Solomon like a magpie to snatch up sparkling treasures of wisdom wherever they may be found. Other authors of these proverbs are identified as Agur and Lemuel (chapters 30 and 31). But whoever the original authors may have been, these wise men throughout are concerned with observing the order of God's world while recognising the disorder introduced by sin – problems of greed, lust, laziness and so on – and in effect saying: 'Look, if the world is made in this way, what is the best way of relating to that world and its Maker who created it? Here are some sayings which are not so much rules for living, but helpful insights as to how we might go about gaining wisdom.' The proverbs (1:7), parables (6:6), sayings (24:14) and riddles (30:18) act as lenses through which life can be observed and wisdom attained. Each day we are faced with hundreds of decisions to be made. Many of these are not simply a matter of right or wrong, but wise and unwise – deciding between the good and the best. How do we go about making these?

However, the way of wisdom is not simply

concerned with making good decisions, but, like
Sister Connie, forming good characters, cultivating
virtues which make us into morally attractive and
spiritually wholesome people. We might well ask:
how are we to go about thinking and living wisely
at the beginning of the twenty-first century? What
should shape our approach to life and issues? The
way of wisdom as enshrined in the book of Proverbs helps us to move in the right direction.

The attributes of wisdom

What characterises wisdom? We are given a
thumbnail portrait of wisdom in 1:1-6:

'The proverbs of Solomon son of David, king of Israel:
    for attaining wisdom and discipline;
        for understanding words of insight;
    for acquiring a disciplined and prudent life,
        doing what is right and just and fair;
    for giving prudence to the simple,
        knowledge and discretion to the young –
    let the wise listen and add to their learning
        and let the discerning get guidance –
    for understanding proverbs and parables,
        the sayings and riddles of the wise.

When I was at school one experiment I found
particularly fascinating was when a white light
was shone through a prism on to a white board so
that the various components of the light were
separated out into the colours of the rainbow. That,
in effect, is what Solomon is doing here – the pure,

white light of wisdom is broken down into several words which in their own way reveal a different facet of wisdom. The first aspect of wisdom in verse 2 is 'discipline' or, as it could be translated, 'education'. The idea is the willingness to submit to instruction and correction. In other words, the wise man or woman is the one who is willing to learn. No one likes a know-all. God certainly doesn't. In fact the word used to describe such a person who can't be told anything is a fool – 'fools despise wisdom and discipline' (v.7b). When you attend church or a Christian meeting, do you do so wanting and willing to learn with a readiness to think, to have your mind and heart expanded? If so, God approves of that:

> 'If you call out for insight
>   and cry aloud for understanding
> and if you look for it as for silver
>   and search for it as for hidden treasure,
> then you will understand the fear of the LORD
>   and find the knowledge of God,
> for the LORD gives wisdom' (2:3-4a).

This wisdom is not handed to someone on a plate – like treasure you dig for it; but also like finding treasure the effort is well worth it. Some very helpful advice to would-be sermon listeners is offered by Charles Swindoll in the form of four 'don'ts' which illustrates this point well. He writes:

Don't assume the subject is dull. When the topic is announced, avoid the habit of thinking, 'I've heard that before' or 'This doesn't apply to me'. Good listeners believe they can learn something from everyone.

Don't criticise before hearing the speaker out. All speakers have faults. If you focus on them, you will miss some profitable points being made....

Don't let your prejudice close your mind. Some subjects are charged with intense emotions. Effective listeners keep an open mind, restraining the tendency to argue or agree until they fully understand the speaker's position in the light of what the Scriptures teach.

Don't waste the advantage which thought has over speech. Remember the gap between speech speed and thought speed. Diligent listeners practice four skills as they mentally occupy themselves:

First, they try to guess the next point.

Second, they challenge the supporting evidence.

Third, they mentally summarise what they have heard.

Fourth, they apply the Scripture at each point.

That is a wise man speaking !

The second aspect of wisdom is 'understanding' (v.2). This means being able to see beneath the surface of things, it's the opposite of being super-ficial. Unfortunately, today we are fascinated with the superficial – someone's image – whether it be in the realm of politics or religion. The wise man or woman, however, is not so easily taken in, he or she will see beyond that to the underlying reality.

Thirdly, wisdom equips us for living a 'prudent life' (v.3). The emphasis here is on the practical nature of wisdom. This is not ivory tower knowledge, it is about living in the real world with real people. Not too long ago I was speaking to someone in industry who was bemoaning the fact that he was being given young graduates to train whose academic qualifications were impeccable but who couldn't make common sense decisions if their lives depended on it. He may have been rather harsh and extreme in his judgment, but certainly in my experience as Chaplain at Keele University I soon discovered that to be clever did not necessarily mean to be sensible!

What is more, according to Solomon a wise man is also a good man, 'doing what is right and just and fair' (v.3b). We tend to separate off ethics from ability. We are therefore all too easily dazzled by someone's academic prowess and are cowered when they pronounce on issues of politics or religion, thinking who are we to question such a great one? But that is to mistake IQ for wise thinking. Take Lord Betrand Russell, for instance. Throughout the 1920s right up to the 1960s he wielded a tremendous influence amongst the intelligentsia of our land. He was considered by some to be the scourge of Christianity; he scorned Christian beliefs and belittled Christian behaviour. It was said that he completed his best work by the age of twenty-four, his great *Principia*

Mathematica. Yet his private life was an absolute mess, littered with infidelity. Here was a product of the Bloomsbury Set who pontificated about the perils of nuclear war, while all but destroying his own children with his cruel and pernicious behaviour. His intellect, which was considerable, had no firm moral base. He was more like the gullible youth described in chapter 7, who is mindlessly led by his hormones into adultery, than the sage who can foresee the moral consequences of self-seeking behaviour. No, the wise man thinks straight and he lives straight.

In verse 4 we are given another aspect of wisdom: 'discretion' – that is the ability to make plans. There is nothing unspiritual in planning, although to hear some people talk today one would think there is. I fear that some are in danger of subscribing to a new form of 'the god of the gaps', so that the Holy Spirit is *only* at work in the spontaneous and immediate.

On one occasion when I turned up at a church to preach, the church official in charge saw me rummaging through my case looking for my sermon notes. Thinking that I had forgotten them he rather excitedly exclaimed, 'Does this mean we are going to hear the Holy Spirit speak through you today?' Why the Holy Spirit should be restricted so that he can only be at work at the moment a sermon is delivered and not in thought-ful and prayerful preparation beforehand, I don't know. The same mistake was made by an actual preacher who used to prepare the first half of his sermons and then freewheel the second half, wishing to 'depend upon the Holy Spirit for inspiration'. One astute lady listening to him one day was perplexed by the change that took place halfway through the sermon. Afterwards she asked the preacher what had happened. So he explained his method to which she replied, 'That is strange. You are a better preacher than the Holy Spirit!'

Surely if God in his wisdom created an orderly world, then we who are made in the image of the Creator should be orderly too. God has created a cosmos not a chaos, so chaos and lack of planning in public worship or the running of a church, far from being signs of spirituality, are indications of carnality. Wisdom, on the other hand, is beautifully ordered.

The last aspect of wisdom is 'knowledge' (v.4). This is not something abstract and detached, but personal and passionate. The wise man gets immersed with the whole of his being in order to understand how the world works, how we tick, so both can be changed for the better. He has a love of life. According to Proverbs it is good to be married, to enjoy the company of friends, to be successful at work, to have money to spend, and so on. There is a life-affirming attitude which is positively encouraged.

Put all of those qualities together – an intelligence

which is disciplined, practical, morally discrim-inating, inventive and emotionally committed, and you have all the makings of a wise person.

The availability of wisdom

Who is this wisdom available to? Just the bright or MENSA candidate? No, wisdom is available to everyone. In Chapter 8, wisdom is portrayed as a beautiful woman who stands at the entrance to a city, the place where everyone has to pass, and she calls out to them to take her:

> 'Does not wisdom call out?
>> Does not understanding raise her voice? On the heights along the way,
>> where the paths meet, she takes her stand: beside the gates leading into the city,
>> at the entrances, she cries aloud:
> "To you, O men, I call out;
>> I raise my voice to all mankind..." ' (8:1-4).

In 1:4 it is the young in particular who are urged to embrace wisdom – to capture them before they learn the hard way and get into bad habits. That is why it is nonsense to say we should not teach children right or wrong or what they should believe but be free to make up their own minds, otherwise we are guilty of indoctrination. The plain fact is, the children will be indoctrinated one way or another from what they see on the television or pick up from their friends. Far better, is it not, that our children learn attractive virtues from Christian parents, or a church school, than behind the bike sheds? Also, wisdom we are told, is for the simple (v.4), literally, the gormless, so they will stop being gullible and become discerning. Wisdom is God's gift for all who are willing to look for it.

The acquisition of wisdom

How, then, do we go about obtaining wisdom? 'The fear of the LORD is the beginning of wisdom' (9:10). True wisdom, which will help us make our way through this complex world, begins by acknowledging the Lord and humbling ourselves before him. It submits to the view that he knows best, and what that is comes to us through his revelation. There is the general revelation of the world which speaks to us of a Creator God, but there is also the special revelation of his Word which makes it clear who he is and what we were made for – this is where we find wisdom.

Wisdom is concerned with making sense of life and being enabled to live the best life possible. If, however, God is left out of the picture, it is like having a jigsaw puzzle, not only with some of the main pieces missing but without a box cover to enable you to see how the pieces are meant to fit together. What you believe will affect the way you behave; 'as a man thinks so he is.'

Where is worldly wisdom likely to lead if you

cut God out? It will be the way of Pol Pot. It was rather pathetic to read the way one national newspaper handled this man's obituary. The writer listed the catalogue of atrocities the leader of the Khmer Rouge committed in Cambodia. On taking over the capital Phnom Phen in 1975, he forced the whole population of two million out into the countryside, many of whom died of starvation. He was responsible for systematically wiping out a third of the Cambodian people. Why, the columnist asked? He tried to answer his own question in terms of a politically unstable country that was ripe for a dictatorship, comparing it with Nazi Germany. What he missed entirely was that it was a young Pol Pot who in the early 1950s went to study under the atheist Jean Paul Sartre in Paris. That is where he learnt the atheism which asserted that life has no meaning and people have no intrinsic value. Seeing the logic of that he set about putting it into practice – in the killing fields of South East Asia.

But the Bible says something else, namely, that there is an all-wise, all-powerful, all-personal God whose wisdom is stamped on the very heavens he has made. We also reflect his wisdom. He has given us minds to think with, hearts to feel with and consciences to wrestle with. The only way we can become rightly related to his world and each other is by being rightly related to him. That is why the Bible in general and Proverbs in particular insist that we shall only start thinking right, feeling right and behaving right when the Creator occupies the centre of our horizons – the reverence of God is the beginning of wisdom. In fact we can now look to one who incarnates the very wisdom of God, the one through whom the world was crafted and for whom it was made, and that someone is Jesus Christ, whom Paul describes as God's wisdom for us (1 Cor. 1: 30).

Are you not captivated by the way Jesus had just the right word to say to the right person at the right time? How he could confound his enemies and bring comfort to his friends? Who not only said good things but did good things because he was good – he was wise? Wouldn't you like to be like him? Jesus says you can be, in increasing measure, for he offers this invitation: 'Take my yolk upon you and learn from me, for I am gentle and humble in heart and you will find rest for your souls' (Matt. 11:29). This is the one who is even greater than Solomon, for he is Solomon's greater son (Luke 11:31).

3

Words, Words, Words

Proverbs 12:13-23

[13]An evil man is trapped by his sinful talk,
    but a righteous man escapes trouble.

[14]From the fruit of his lips a man is filled with good
                                    things
    as surely as the work of his hands rewards him.

[15]The way of a fool seems right to him,
    but a wise man listens to advice.

[16]A fool shows his annoyance at once
    but a prudent man overlooks an insult.

[17]A truthful witness gives honest testimony,
    but a false witness tells lies.

[18]Reckless words pierce like a sword,
    but the tongue of the wise brings healing.

[19]Truthful lips endure forever,
    but a lying tongue lasts only a moment.

[20]There is deceit in the hearts of those who plot evil,
    but joy for those who promote peace.

[21]No harm befalls the righteous,
    but the wicked have their fill of trouble.

[22]The LORD detests lying lips,
　　but he delights in men who are truthful.

[23]A prudent man keeps his knowledge to himself,
　　but the heart of fools blurts out folly.

Proverbs 24:26
An honest answer
　　is like a kiss on the lips.

Proverbs 10:19
When words are many, sin is not absent,
　　but he who holds his tongue is wise.

Proverbs 18:8
The words of a gossip are like choice morsels;
　　they go down to a man's inmost parts.

Proverbs 15:23
A man finds joy in giving an apt reply –
　　and how good is a timely word!

Proverbs 15:1
A gentle answer turns away wrath,
　　but a harsh word stirs up anger.

'I have a dream today,' so runs one of the most famous lines from perhaps one of the most memorable speeches of the twentieth century, the speech delivered by Dr. Martin Luther King at the Washington Memorial during the Civil Rights March of 1963. It was a stirring speech, reaching into the hearts and minds of millions throughout the United States. Some thirty years earlier, another charismatic figure gave a speech, someone who also had a dream, a somewhat different dream, more of a nightmare. His name was Adolf Hitler. In the 1930s he gave rousing speeches to crowds gathered in their thousands by torchlight, the reverberations of which were to be felt throughout the entire world.

What is the moral of that? It is this: words are powerful. Those seemingly inconsequential marks on a paper or noises emanating from our larynges are invested with almost magical powers which far exceed their natural status. Words have the capacity to create or destroy, uplift or depress, heal or hurt, excite or bore. Of all the creatures on this planet human beings alone have ability for sophisticated language. We use words to think with, to inform with, to express our feelings with and also to create with. Just think of it, an author can bring about populated imaginary worlds within the minds of thousands simply by telling a story. What is more, by words we can speak into existence new states of affairs, what the linguistic philosopher J. L. Austin called 'performatives'. When a bride and groom, therefore, utter the words 'I will,' they are not *describing* marriage, they are actually bringing a marriage into being. A brand new family unit is formed by two little words.

The Power of Words

It is also as linguistic beings that we reflect the biblical conviction that we are made in God's image, for, however we may think of God, he is supremely the God of the Word. God creates by a word, 'In the beginning God created the heavens and the earth. God said, "Let there be ... and there was."' He also relates to us by a word. In Eden God spoke to the man a loving word of command: 'You may eat of any tree in the garden bar one, for that will harm you.' He also reveals by a word; the phrase, 'Thus says the Lord', appears over 3,000 times in the Old Testament. But what is more, God saves by a Word – the Word of the gospel of Jesus Christ in whose person all of these things come together: 'In the beginning was the Word, and the Word was with God, and the Word was God. Through him all things were made.... The Word became flesh and dwelt amongst us. He came so that all who believed in his name, should be given the right to become children of God.' So writes the apostle John in the opening verses of his Gospel.

Therefore, it should come as no surprise to us that given the power and importance of words, the book of Proverbs should give advice on how we are to *use* words. Such a use begins by listening to the words of wisdom itself: 'Listen, my sons, to a father's instruction; pay attention and gain understanding.... do not forget *my* words or swerve from them' (4:1, 5).

The Work of Words

Have you ever wondered how words work, how they become so powerful in shaping our thought life – our beliefs, values and so our actions? Someone who spent much time considering this question was the late Professor Donald MacKay, who was not only a brain scientist of international repute at Keele University but also a committed Christian thinker and writer. The way he tried to explain how messages – words – affect our brains was by using the following illustration: In a railway shunting yard there is a box of levers. When the levers are set up in a certain pattern, the yard is ready to deal with the traffic in a corresponding way. Even if there are not trains in the yard at that moment, it is ready to do business, sending trains this way or that if they were to come. If you change the switches, the ability to cope with the traffic will also change. Now, putting it crudely, he said, this is a picture of what goes on in our heads when we communicate with each other. Words are like specially designed tools which change the switch settings of our brains. Not that they necessarily *make* us *do* things, but they get us ready to act differently – they affect what he termed 'our conditional states of readiness.' So, if someone were to say to you, 'I invite you to a roast beef lunch next Sunday,' and you believed him, your brain state would be changed, ready to act in response to that message. Accordingly, you may decide to cancel your planned meal, apologise because you already have some other engagement on that day or whatever. Even just imagining it could have effects. So, you might be so passionate about roast beef that the very prospect starts you salivating, or if you are vegetarian, you are so appalled at the idea you feel physically sick. The point is this, wrote MacKay: 'No communication is ever *neutral – it will have an effect.* Thinking is not neutral; looking or listening are not neutral; imagining is not neutral; even asking a question is not neutral at the level at which our brains operate.'[1] We are changed for good or ill.

If it is the case that messages shape our brain states – affecting our beliefs and so how we behave – then the way we use words has very profound implications. This is where God's wisdom, as detailed in the book of Proverbs, which we have

1. Donald MacKay, *Human Science and Human Dignity*, Hodder and Stoughton, 1979, p. 80..

defined as God's truth, comes in, to enable God's people to live in God's world, God's way.

The Use of Words

How, then, are words to be used?

First of all we must make sure they are *true*: 'An honest answer is like a kiss on the lips' (Prov. 24:26); 'With his mouth the godless destroys his neighbour, but through knowledge the righteous escape' (Prov. 11:9); 'The LORD detests lying lips, but he delights in men who are truthful' (Prov. 12:22). Now, why does God do that? What is so important about telling the truth? For one thing it reflects the character of God: he is truth, dead straight in all his dealings with us. He doesn't pull the wool over our eyes and neither should we with others.

But also to engage in deceit – although we wouldn't call it that nowadays, we would use more high sounding terms like, 'being economical with the truth' – is to damage ourselves and other people. And it happens in this way: by perverting the truth, even slightly, is to shape the way other people see things and are prepared to act on things that don't correspond with reality as God has made it. Thinking back to the illustration of the switch settings of our brain; lies set the switches in a pattern which will prepare people to act in a way which is out of kilter with the way things actually are. And so we shouldn't be surprised if they are harmed as a result. Let's take the lie, which has been portrayed as truth in our society since the early 1960s, that 'sexual freedom is good.' That message has been put over in so many different ways – through books, films, magazines, sex education in schools, songs and so on. It is a message which has shaped the way people think and act. What has come in its wake? More teenage pregnancies, sexual disease, and marital breakdown, not less.

A news item appeared on the main evening news which gripped me. It concerned university students who in order to cope with the financial burdens of study were becoming involved in prostitution, young men as well as women. This was put over by the reporters as a shocking thing. In one sense it is. But we might well ask: why the big surprise? Given the message that has been pounding away over the last thirty years that sex is essentially for pleasure rather than for bonding and reproduction, then there is a certain logic in getting paid for it as well. You see, the messages we receive will shape the way we behave. And so, by Christians promoting the *truth* about the way God has made the world and how we are to act in it, we help people to live healthily and not damage themselves and others in the process of living a lie. That is why truth is important.

Secondly, words should be *few*: 'When words are many, sin is not absent, but he who holds his tongue is wise' (Prov. 10:19). That may mean, be careful of the man with the gift of the gab for he may well be trying to pull a fast one on you. Or it could mean, the more you say unthinkingly you are bound to say something which will be wrong, sinful, whereas a wise person will weigh carefully his words before he opens his mouth – 'Think before you speak.' It doesn't always follow that the more the words the better the quality of the message. For instance, the Lord's prayer is made up of 56 words, the 23rd Psalm 118 words, the Ten Commandments 297 words, the US Department of Agriculture's Order on the price of cabbage 15,629 words!

Thirdly, our words should be *pure*: 'Reckless words pierce like a sword, but the tongue of the wise brings healing' (Prov. 12:18). What we say should be wholesome, uplifting, life-enhancing, the exact opposite to that which is vulgar, base, and demeaning. Words in the mouth of a Christian should be attractive and good; the foul mouth is the characteristic of a fool. And even when a rebuke has to be given, it is more like a scalpel in the hands of a skilful surgeon, building up a person rather than thoughtless words which are like a sword destroying the person. Can we ask ourselves, how pure are our words? Is there a loveliness about our speech which attracts people, pours oil on troubled waters? Or is our speech negative, cynical, destructive? The latter particularly shows itself in gossip: 'The words of a gossip are like choice morsels; they go down to a man's inmost parts' (Prov. 18:8) – that is they are so fascinating, that we take them in deeply and the damage is done. How many Christians, and indeed whole churches, have been effectively destroyed by gossip? The late Alan Redpath once suggested that any gossip which comes our way should be subject to the following test summed up in the acronym THINK: T – is it true? H – is it helpful? I – is it inspiring? N – is it necessary? K – is it kind?

This naturally leads us to another important point regarding pure messages, that it applies not just to giving them but receiving them. We are to guard ourselves in *what* we hear: 'Above all else, guard your heart, for it is the wellspring of life. Put away perversity from your mouth; keep corrupt talk far from your lips' (Prov. 4:23-24).

To quote Professor Donald MacKay: 'All our evidence suggests that human communication, mechanism and meaning are so inextricably interwoven that by communicating with a man you cannot avoid effecting physical changes in him, some of which may not be reversible, just as surely and as fatefully as if you laid your hands on him.'[2] He argues that information has effects on our brains which are just as material as, say,

---

2. MacKay, Ibid, p. 87.

arsenic or alcohol. It's amazing, he says, that we rightly have laws which restrict environmental pollution and yet hardly any which limit mental pollution – what appears on our TV, for instance! 'Ah,' responds the cynic, 'it is a myth that our behaviour is affected by such things. No one watching a violent movie goes out to commit violence.' The cause and effect relationship between messages and actions might not be so straightforward but are nonetheless real as born out by the neuroscientific evidence of MacKay as well as by disturbing events.

According to the *Education Reporter,* a Californian school district participated in a project in creative writing. The children were to imagine coming to school on a 'misty, foggy morning' to find a strange car in the field, with the teacher's voice coming from the car. The tone of the opening line was one of mystery. Do you know what the children wrote? One story was about his teacher holding the class hostage with a machine gun. One was about the teacher kidnapping a child. Another about the teacher planning to assassinate the head. Sometimes the teacher was the victim; one wrote about taping his teacher's mouth and pointing a gun to her head. One even wrote about his teacher being brutally raped. The children were only eight-nine years old. Should we therefore be so surprised but no less shocked at the publicised shootings that took place recently in two schools in America? Or the recent rape in this country of a five-year-old by a twelve-year-old? As they say, 'Rubbish in, rubbish out.' It might be worth asking: Do we know what our children and grandchildren are watching? Are we aware of the messages they are receiving? We wouldn't dream of letting them drink a bottle of bleach, would we? Yet messages that come their way can be just as damaging. 'Guard your heart,' says the wise man.

But fourthly, our words should be *apt*; right words, spoken in the right way, for the right occasion: 'A man finds joy in giving an apt reply – and how good is a timely word' (Prov. 15:23); 'A gentle answer turns away wrath, but a harsh word stirs up anger' (Prov. 15:1). One of the dangers we run in communicating in a sloppy way is misunderstanding. Sometimes this can be amusing. So we have the following quotes from actual church publications: 'Don't let worry kill you – let the church help'; 'This being Easter Sunday, we will ask Mrs. Lewis to come forward and lay an egg on the altar'; and this is my favourite: 'The preacher for next week will be found hanging on the notice board.'

But choice of the wrong word or words being said in the wrong way can have serious results. Here is a conversation between a husband and wife:

He says, 'Will you call the electrician?'

She replies, 'I will if you ask me in a nice tone of voice.'

'I did ask in a nice way,' he exclaims.

'But you always whine when you want me to do something,' she says.

So finally he explodes, 'If you don't want to do it, just say so.'

Do you see what has happened? The *actual words* of the husband were quite civil, but the *tone* indicated a reprimand. *How* we say a thing can be just as important as what we say.

Developing this point Professor MacKay writes:

Inconsistency between verbal and non-verbal aspects can be fully as disastrous to total function as purely verbal contradiction. The man who purports to lead prayers to God in a tone that means 'Here's what it says in the book,' or 'now, then, folks, what do you say in response?' is emitting self-contradictory nonsense. A preacher who talks about God as if he had forgotten that he was in God's very presence may say nothing theologically false, and yet destroy the whole communicative fabric of his sermon.[3]

Words are a wonderful gift of God with tremendous power for good or evil. The responsibility we have to use them properly is great. Could it be with this in mind that Jesus uttered one of his most solemn warnings: 'I tell

3. MacKay, Ibid., p. 99.

you that men will have to give account on the day of judgement for every careless word they have spoken. For by your words you will be acquitted, and by your words you will be condemned' (Matt. 12:36-37)?

4

Whose Life is it Anyway?
Psalm 139

Psalm 139

[1]O LORD, you have searched me
  and you know me.
[2]You know when I sit and when I rise;
  you perceive my thoughts from afar.
[3]You discern my going out and my lying down;
  you are familiar with all my ways.
[4]Before a word is on my tongue
  you know it completely, O LORD.

[5]You hem me in – behind and before;
  you have laid your hand upon me.
[6]Such knowledge is too wonderful for me,
  too lofty for me to attain.

[7]Where can I go from your Spirit?
  Where can I flee from your presence?
[8]If I go up to the heavens, you are there;
  if I make my bed in the depths, you are there.
[9]If I rise on the wings of the dawn,
  if I settle on the far side of the sea,
[10]even there your hand will guide me,
  your right hand will hold me fast.

[11]If I say, "Surely the darkness will hide me
  and the light become night around me,"
[12]even the darkness will not be dark to you;
  the night will shine like the day,
  for darkness is as light to you.

[13]For you created my inmost being;
  you knit me together in my mother's womb.

¹⁴I praise you because I am fearfully and wonderfully
                                                made;
    your works are wonderful,
    I know that full well.
¹⁵My frame was not hidden from you
    when I was made in the secret place.
When I was woven together in the depths of the earth,
    ¹⁶your eyes saw my unformed body.
All the days ordained for me
    were written in your book
    before one of them came to be.

¹⁷How precious to me are your thoughts, O God!
    How vast is the sum of them!
¹⁸Were I to count them,
    they would outnumber the grains of sand.
When I awake,
    I am still with you.

¹⁹If only you would slay the wicked, O God!
    Away from me, you bloodthirsty men!
²⁰They speak of you with evil intent;
    Your adversaries misuse your name.
²¹ Do I not hate those who hate you, O LORD,
    and abhor those who rise up against you?
²²I have nothing but hatred for them;
    I count them my enemies.

²³Search me, O God, and know my heart;
    test me and know my anxious thoughts.
²⁴See if there is any offensive way in me,
    and lead me in the way everlasting.

Whether it be a seven-week-old foetus in the womb or a seventy-year-old ailing man terminally ill from cancer, as the future of each is considered, the question is sometimes voiced, 'Whose life is it anyway?' The implication being that someone, somewhere, has the right to choose the termination of a life.

The common perception of the Christian position on the matter of the sanctity of life is that it is an absolute ethic; that is, human life should never be taken away and should be preserved at all costs. Whatever the basis of this common perception it is in fact a *mis*perception. Although the sanctity of life is of a fundamental value, it is not an absolute value. Not only did the Lord Jesus consider the giving over of his own life for that which he considered to be of greater worth – the redemption of his people – he also urged upon his own followers that losing one's life for the sake of the kingdom of God is no bad thing, as is well expounded in Matthew 10, for instance. As the theologian Karl Barth put it, for the Christian, 'life is no second god'. While the sanctity of human life may seem quite self-evident to many, the fact is, as a principle it has been used both for *and* against capital punishment, abortion and euthanasia.

Tainted Values

One of the problems we face as we consider this subject is that we approach it with our views already 'coloured'. Often without even being aware of it, we adopt ideas of human rights, personhood, quality of life and so on which, to put it mildly, have less grounding in Scripture and are more rooted in the well-fertilised soil of a post-enlightenment world – a view which is now falling apart under the onslaught of post-modernism. For example, it is now taken as given that we have a 'right to choose'; indeed in the cases of abortion and euthanasia it is placed on a higher scale of values (if such a scale exists) than the right to life itself. As with most heresies, religious or secular, this is a Christian truth gone wrong; like multiplying cancer cells, such perverted ideas engulf that which is healthy. The Christian tradition of freedom of the will – however limited that will is by original sin and circumstances – has practically devoured everything else. Whereas the Bible, and indeed pagans like Aristotle, would consider it right to ask the question '*What* should we choose?' – in other words choice is linked to other moral questions. Today individual worth is seen almost entirely in terms of the fact *that* we choose.

Stanley Hauerwas of Duke University points out that what is happening in many schools and colleges is that ethics is being treated solely as a matter of individual decision making. The goal of such moral education is to teach students to make up their own minds. The problem is, says Hauerwas, that 'Most students don't have minds worth making up.' That is, their minds have not been trained in the great principles of truth and justice which have been the foundation of Western culture for centuries. Instead they are told to look within and go with the flow of their feelings. They have no moral reference point by which they can chart the directions of the decisions they make. To modify the dictum of Descartes 'I choose therefore I am.' The sociologist Peter Berger has called this 'The Heretical Imperative'. There was a time when heresy was considered to be a matter of going down the wrong path; now it is heretical not to go down any path at all.

The name of the game is 'autonomy' – doing what *I* want. The Christian would view freedom somewhat differently, tying it in with what God wills, the divine ought. So Karl Barth expresses this thought in the following way: 'True freedom is not a choice between alternatives; our one freedom is obedience to the will of God. What we call freedom as 'free will' is not freedom. We are free if we agree with God, otherwise we are prisoners. The liberty of free will is sin!'

Rootless ethics

However, when God is evacuated from the picture such that there are no moral absolutes (save this moral absolute – the right to choose), then it makes little difference in which direction we go – to save life or to take it. But one can appreciate the logic that if quality of life and value of life are inextricably linked to the ability to choose, then those who *cannot choose*, whether an unborn baby or a comatose victim, forfeit the right to protection. After all, why protect that which has less value than ourselves? One can also see how if dignity is defined in terms of choosing, then the one last dignified act that a person may make is to exercise the ultimate choice in ending one's life, or demanding that it be ended for them, thus transferring the moral obligation on to someone else.

There are three basic biblical principles which should inform the way we might view aright the question of the sanctity of life.

1. Life is a gift

When we go back to Genesis 2:7 we see that it is God who breathes into man the breath of life. Unlike the bringing about of the rest of creation, there is an intimacy here, almost the imparting of something God-like to man. This gift is precious, reflecting as it does something of God himself –

men and women are made in his image (Gen. 1:27; 9:6). To take away this life in a deliberate act of malice, as Genesis 9 and the sixth commandment make plain is murder, and in some measure marks an attack on the Creator whose image humans bear. In other words, this gift of human life contains something of the Giver, like the portrait of a loving parent. And so to deface or destroy this portrait would at the very least be an act of appalling disrespect. In the words of the ethicist Paul Ramsey it would be 'to throw the gift of life back in the face of the Giver'. The value people have is God-given, not man-determined. Just as we are simply called to recognise the beauty of a sunset, so we are called to recognise the value of a human being. However, such a recognition may well have to be *informed* because of our faulty moral perception due to sin. Think, for example, of how until relatively recently black people were not recognised as human by some white people. This means that the Christian will be suspicious of accepting other morally dubious criteria for determining the value of human life, whether it be 'biological quality' or 'usefulness'. Within the grand sweep of Scripture life is seen as a gift to be received with gratitude, in contrast to death which stands as an 'abnormal normal' in a fallen world.

2. Life is on loan

The gracious nature of life as a gift to be received, rather than a right to be asserted, is focused for us in that well-known response of Job: 'Naked I came from my mother's womb, and naked I shall depart. The LORD gave and the LORD has taken away; may the name of the LORD be praised' (Job 1:21). The life giver is also the life taker. Since life is on loan as it were, it is not ours to do with as we please; it is something which belongs to God and so calls to us to use that life in responsible freedom in the service and praise of God. It could therefore be argued that to choose death, our own or that of another as an end in itself with divine sanction, is to usurp the place of God. To the question so often raised, 'Whose life is it anyway?', the Christian's answer would be, 'It is God's.' But this does run counter to the prevailing assumption of our age. This is well illustrated by the response of one theological student to the writings of Karl Barth who insisted on this principle that 'life is on loan from God'. The response was simply: 'What I really don't like about him (Barth) is that he seems to think that our lives are not our own.' Autonomy, the belief that we and we alone decide what to do, is the order of the day. It is the age-old question first raised in Eden, 'Who is to be God?'

3. Life is to be redeemed

God's commands are not arbitrary. They are grounded in his moral character, what he is like within himself, and orientated towards his purposes for his creation. What is the goal of creation? It is the kingdom of God, God's saving rule through his Son Jesus Christ, which will be consummated at the end of time.

Christ came to redeem us from the curse of the law (Gal. 3:13), to destroy the one who holds the power over death and to release those whose lives are held in fear of death (Heb. 2:14-15). Death is the final enemy which one day will be destroyed (1 Cor. 15:26), and what will be the case at the end of time, is tasted in time, in Jesus' own ministry (e.g. John 11) and supremely in his resurrection (1 Cor. 15:20). Here is the model and basis for medical care – the person and work of Christ who sought to bring healing, relief and life. It is true that the Christian has an ambivalent attitude towards death – seeing it both as an enemy and as a release and therefore gateway into glory (1 Cor. 15:56; 2 Cor. 5:1ff; Phil. 1:21f). Nonetheless, the overall direction of Scripture is in viewing death in negative terms, with a positive emphasis on caring for the sick and needy, however costly.

As someone has put it, the kingdom of God inaugurated by the resurrection is 'creation healed'. It is this understanding of God's perfect rule in Christ being the goal of creation which gives us a clue as to what is meant by the term 'image of God'.

Christ centred ethics

As we look to Jesus, whom we are told is 'the image of the invisible God' (Col 1:15), what do we see which is particularly 'God-like'? Is it not how he relates?

First, how he relates to his Father: 'The Son can do nothing by himself; he can do only what he sees his Father doing, because whatever the Father does the Son also does' (John 5:19). Second, how he relates to others in serving, healing and teaching. And third, how he relates to the world as in stilling the storm (Mark 4:35-41; compare with Psalm 89:9: 'You rule over the surging sea; when its waves mount up, you still them.' Could this have been behind the disciples' vexed question, 'Who is this? Even the wind and waves obey him'). In other words, in Jesus we see what man was originally meant to be, representing God to the world by ruling it responsibly (Gen. 1: 26-28). All of this, of course, will be completed and consummated when Christ returns (Heb. 2: 5-9).

It is this understanding of men and women being in God's image which gives the individual great value, but it is a *relational value*. The image of God is not so much something *in* us; but something expressed *between* us – between us and God, between us and each other, and between us and creation. That image marred by sin is now being renewed amongst those who are redeemed (Col. 3:10: 'and have put on the new self – which is being renewed in knowledge in the image of its Creator' – the context being how we relate to one another).

If we follow this through, then we have a perspective on the question of the sanctity of life that has been neglected by evangelicals in the past. Traditionally it has been argued that one does not take away human life in the womb by abortion or prematurely at the entrance to the tomb by euthanasia because the person is made in the image of God, and so is of supreme value and worth. While not wishing to deny this aspect as far as it goes, in addition we should also be pursuing the question as to whether to take away life at the rate of three abortions a minute in this country (over 90% of which are on social grounds), or at the rate of 9% of all deaths by euthanasia in the Netherlands (which if transferred to this country would be the equivalent of 1,000 per week as a percentage of the total population), is the sort of activity someone should be doing who is made in God's image? When we see in the One who uniquely bears the image of the invisible God someone who restores life rather than takes it away, who will not break a bruised reed or snuff out a smouldering wick, then are we not given some very clear indicators of what sort of responses we should be making as those who are to express God's image in the way we relate to one another?

This relational understanding of how we are to approach the issue of the sanctity of life helps us avoid becoming bogged down in abstract notions such as 'personhood' – is this a person whom I am to accord the same rights of protection as myself? The fact is, we care for someone not because of some abstract concept, but because we are thrown together in covenantal relationships. I relate to this one as a father, brother, son, mother, daughter, minister, doctor and so on. These are relationships which are meant to be based upon trust, responsibility and obligation. If a woman miscarries, especially late, she feels she has not lost a conceptus, but *her baby*. Even after death and one is still holding the hand of the loved one, we recognise that the body still echoes the person. As Stanley Hauerwas subtitles one of his essays, 'He may not be much of a person, but he is still my uncle Charlie.' The identity and worth of an individual is grounded in their relationship to others. Even if no one else were around to love and care for a particular individual, this does not mean that their worth is on any ultimate scale of values reduced, for there is still one who watches over them and relates to them in covenant love –

the Creator-Redeemer God – a truth which Psalm 139 expresses so beautifully and profoundly. Note how the emphasis is on God as the one who oversees his work of creating and sustaining the individual, even mapping out the individual's life story. It is how *he* relates to us which gives us value as well as pointing to how *we* are to relate to others:

> For you created my inmost being;
>   you knit me together in my mother's womb.
> I praise you because I am fearfully and
>   wonderfully made;
>   your works are wonderful,
>   I know that full well.
> My frame was not hidden from you
>   when I was made in the secret place.
> When I was woven together in the depths of the
> earth,
>   your eyes saw my unformed body.
> All the days ordained for me
>   were written in your book
>   before one of them came to be.
>
> How precious to me are your thoughts, O God!
>   How vast is the sum of them!
> Were I to count them,
>   they would outnumber the grains of sand.
> When I awake,
>   I am still with you
>
>   (Psalm 139:13-18).

5

A matter of
life and death
Euthanasia

Proverbs 3:29

Do not plot harm against your neighbour,
    who lives trustfully near you.

Proverbs 9: 10-11

[10]The fear of the LORD is the beginning of wisdom,
    and knowledge of the Holy One is understanding.
[11]For through me your days will be many,
    and years will be added to your life.

Proverbs 10:27

The fear of the LORD adds length to life,
    but the years of the wicked are cut short.

Proverbs 14:32

When calamity comes, the wicked are brought
        down,
    but even in death the righteous have a refuge.

Proverbs 24:11-12

[11]Rescue those being led away to death;
    hold back those staggering toward slaughter.
[12]If you say, 'But we knew nothing about this,'
    does not he who weighs the heart perceive it?
Does not he who guards your life know it?
    Will he not repay each person according to what
        he has done?

They call him Dr. Death. His real name is Dr. Jack Kevorkian. Until his licence to practise medicine had been withdrawn, he achieved some notoriety in the United States by inventing a suicide machine. His whole purpose was to help people kill themselves, to exercise what some would consider to be the ultimate right to 'die with dignity'. The organization in the States which seeks to legalise this activity called euthanasia is known as the Hemlock society. It has even listed leading churchmen to aid its cause. So the Reverend John Pridonoff has gone on record as saying that euthanasia is OK because God wouldn't want people to suffer. When a local reporter challenged him on this, asking 'Isn't the Bible against suicide?' he simply replied, 'But there are lots of things in the Bible we've grown beyond as a society.'

In Britain there is an all-party euthanasia group which claims the support of over a hundred MPs. If you will excuse the pun, euthanasia is an issue which refuses to die.

'Euthanasia' literally means 'dying well', and as such is a fairly neutral term. However, in recent years, largely through the work of the Voluntary Euthanasia Society (formerly EXIT), it has taken on a more specialised meaning. Put simply, euthanasia refers to 'medically assisted suicide'. A more precise definition would be, 'The deliberate bringing about of the death of a human being as part of the medical care being given him or her.' Immediately, this might strike many people as odd. For it may well be argued that there is an internal contradiction involved; how can bringing about someone's death be conceived as being *part* of the medical care offered? Surely to terminate life is to terminate the medical care also; it can't therefore be part of it.

Advocates of euthanasia often muddy the ethical waters by raising the question, 'Should life be preserved at all costs?', and assume that if the answer is 'no,' then this legitimizes euthanasia.

Two things need to be said in response.

First, even Christians who would place a high value on the sanctity of human life would not advocate preserving life at *all* costs. One only has to think of the extraordinary lengths taken (which were politically motivated) to preserve the 'lives' of Tito and Franco in their last moments. This would not be considered justified, medically or ethically.

Secondly, there is a world of difference in terms of *intention* between deliberately *shortening a life (euthanasia)* and *choosing not to prolong the dying process* unnecessarily. The former involves the intention of killing, the latter the intention of not prolonging the dying. The difference between them is morally important and the two should not be confused.

Signs of the times

We must realise that already events have taken place which have helped pave the way to making euthanasia acceptable within the collective consciousness of our society. In 1992, Dr. Nigel Cox was prosecuted for the attempted murder of Lilian Boyes, a long-standing patient of his who was suffering from severe rheumatoid arthritis. Her life expectancy was short and she asked Dr. Cox to end it for her. At first he refused. But then he gave her a lethal injection of potassium chloride and she died within minutes. He was found guilty and received a twelve-month suspended sentence. He was also reprimanded by the General Medical Council but continues in practice today. This is an example of voluntary euthanasia, assisting the death of someone who has requested it.

A few years earlier, a Downs syndrome baby, John Pearson, was given a deliberate overdose of dihydrocodeine by his doctor, Leonard Arthur. The doctor was acquitted and again treated leniently by the medical authorities. This is an example of non-voluntary euthanasia – a case when the sick patient is not able to request death but the decision is taken on their behalf.

Some may ask: what is the problem? Don't people have a right to do with their lives as they choose? If you were to see an animal in pain with no hope of recovery and you had a gun in your hand you would put it out of its misery, wouldn't you? So why not offer the same compassionate way out for a fellow human being? When put like that, the arguments for euthanasia seem so compelling, brimful with common sense. But is there an alternative – a third way between allowing people to suffer needlessly and ending their lives prematurely? The Christian would reply there is, and it is the way of wisdom.

In the Book of Proverbs we are given insights which help us begin to get this important subject into some kind of focus. As we have already seen, wisdom is essentially God's truth, enabling God's people to live in God's world, God's way.

Evangelical thinking

It is all too easy to respond to this issue emotionally. But wisdom is all to do with thinking evangelically, that is biblically. In fact there are three questions which biblical wisdom raises which, when taken together, would guide us on this subject of euthanasia. There are questions of principle, questions of motive, and questions of consequences.

Questions of Principle

There are three principles which are relevant as to whether medically assisted suicide is something we ought to be encouraging as a society.

First there is the principle of *love*.

As we have seen, those in favour of euthanasia

argue it is the most loving thing to do in some cases. Granny is in pain, you have a hypodermic in your bag, why not do the most loving thing? But to borrow a phrase coined by Professor Joad, 'it all depends on what you mean' by love.

There are two words we find in Proverbs translated 'love' which often mean different things. There is the word *aheb* which tends to mean being fond of something; so 12:1, 'Whoever loves discipline *loves* knowledge.' It is affection. And that is how we tend to think of love; little more than a feeling. The other word is *hesed*, which can be translated steadfast love, unfailing love, indeed, grace. It is the word most often used to describe God's love. This is a love of the will which takes into account what in the long term will be the best for a person, or society as a whole, and what is morally right. So Proverbs 14:22 'Those who plan what is good show love (*hesed*) and faithfulness.' Now just think of how God expressed this type of love to Israel. It was compassionate – moved with pity as he saw his people in slavery in Egypt and he took steps to do something positive. It is creative – when Israel kept failing, God didn't just give up on them saying, 'Let me put them out of their misery and me out of mine, so I will get rid of them and find another nation with a bit more potential.' No, he creatively found ways to correct them, teach them, woo them on to better things. It is also costly –

sticking by these people through thick and thin, feeling the pain of spurned love and patiently going on with them. As we are made to be like God, so our love is to be like his, not taking the short-term, easy way out, but the more costly creative way forward.

The second principle is *justice*, not showing bias against certain classes of people. Therefore, in Proverbs 1:3 we are told that wisdom is for 'doing what is right and just and fair'. Throughout Scripture, God is concerned with championing the cause of the powerless and unrepresented in society – what we may call the 'poor.' So Proverbs 14:31, 'He who oppresses the poor shows contempt for their Maker.' Certainly in the case of non-voluntary euthanasia, where perhaps a little Downs syndrome baby or a frail elderly relative has their life cut short simply because they are classed as having no hope or potential for a so-called quality life, does seem to smack of injustice, a bias against the ill and the aged, what may be called infirmism or ageism.

Thirdly, there is the principle of *life*. Life is a good gift of Wisdom, 'Long life is in her right hand' (3:16). The very creation of mankind flows out of God's loving wisdom; in 8:31, Wisdom having done its creating work is said to 'rejoice in the whole of mankind'. In another wisdom book, Job 1:21, we read that it is 'the LORD who gave and the LORD who has taken away.' Life is a gift of God on loan to us, not to do with as we please but in a way that pleases him. By way of contrast, death is generally seen as a bad thing, a curse resulting from our sinful rebellion: 'The fear of the LORD adds length to life, but the years of the wicked are cut short' (10:27). The whole concept of the sanctity of life which has undergirded our medical profession for years is based upon this biblical view – human life is sacred – and that is why it is so serious to take away life without divine sanction. It is in short murder, taking the place of God.

Furthermore, the Christian would wish to contend that it is in Wisdom incarnate that we find all of these principles expressed perfectly, that is, in the life of Jesus. He is the one who shows creative love – healing at personal cost to himself and in a variety of ways. He didn't just pronounce *en masse* for people to be healed, he dealt with them all individually and differently, which was taxing and tiring. He was impartial too in his care for the sick; whether they be Jew or non-Jew, male, female, child, adult, he tendered to them all, not writing any off as beyond the pale. Also in Jesus we see God as the great life giver, who himself died in order to redeem us from the curse of death, so that by *his* wounds we are healed (1 Pet. 2:24). Therefore, if Jesus is all that God intended man to be, as well as God himself, then surely how he treated the sick is how we are to treat them.

Also, we need to take into account the question of motives. Proverbs 16:2 says, 'All a man's ways seem innocent to him, but motives are weighed by the LORD.' The point is this: we may convince ourselves that the early death of a patient is for their good, while all the while other ulterior motives are at work. Could it not be that it is for our self-interest we urge euthanasia? For *we* don't want to bear the emotional toil of seeing a loved one suffer. A friend of mine who teaches ethics to medical students at Oxford has remarked that one of the things he has real problems with is medics who can't cope with death and see it as failure. One result is an attraction to the idea of euthanasia as an answer to this. So by the doctor supervising death, there is some psychological comfort that it is part of the treatment, enduring total control.

But perhaps more of a factor will be the economic motive for euthanasia. With the current financial crisis in health care in Britain, coupled with an increasing elderly population, it would not be too difficult envisaging us reaching a situation where euthanasia of the elderly or terminally ill could be seen as a means of easing the financial burden. Are these noble motives which God would weigh favourably? The answer must be a resounding 'no'.

Further, wisdom would have us think of the wider consequences of a euthanasia policy. In

Proverbs 1:4 we are told that wisdom gives discretion, that is the ability to plan and foresee consequences. Here are just a few.

Proverbs 3:29 says, 'Do not plot to harm your neighbour who lives *trust*fully near you.' We need to ask: how would euthanasia affect the doctor-patient relationship? In the Netherlands where voluntary euthanasia is an accepted part of medical practice, in 1990 there were 3,700 deaths by euthanasia, 1,030 of which were non-voluntary. As you can imagine, this has had an un-nerving effect amongst the elderly there. A few moments reflection reveals 'Why is this nice doctor who has been giving me pink pills for the last two months, now giving me a yellow pill to cure me or kill me?' would not be an unreasonable thought. Wouldn't you feel more than a little nervous in such a nursing home? The doctor/patient relationship is based on trust. Euthanasia replaces trust with suspicion. Also, should doctors and nurses whose traditional motivation is based on striving to save lives be put in a position where they would legally be required to take away lives? How loving and just would that be for *them?* The psychological strain would be considerable, witness the stress on the performing of abortions. What is more, there would be a gradual erosion of motivation for care: with increasing demands on the health care system and less money, the easy option towards euthanasia would be so attractive.

But let us ask: what sort of message would widespread acceptance of euthanasia send to society as a whole about the value of the elderly and infirm? It has been suggested that there is a link between abortion on demand and child abuse – if we treat our young in this way in the womb as being of little value, and inconvenience perhaps, then why not when they are out of the womb? How long, then, would it take for similar attitudes to be engendered towards the elderly? So-called Granny bashing would become more common. Actions create and reinforce attitudes.

Is there a third way?

Well, there are basically three courses of action open to us when dealing with a terminally ill patient. They are represented in the diagram below.

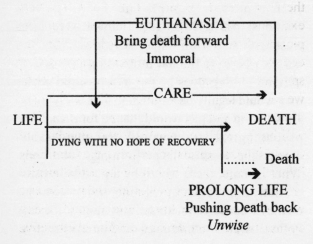

First, there is euthanasia which is immoral. Secondly, there is the prolonging of the dying process artificially in a way that is disproportionate to any advantage that might be gained by the patient, i.e. pursuing *futile* treatment. This may not always be immoral but it certainly can be unwise and distressing. A minister I know once visited a hospital patient who was linked up with tubes and electrodes and was expected to live only a very short time. At one point visitors were asked to leave while the nurse quickly administered some treatment. She said afterwards with more than a hint of desperation in her voice, 'I nearly lost her then.' Why, they wondered, wasn't the patient allowed to die peacefully? In fact, she lived one more day.

There is, however, a third way and that is in the provision of palliative care and relief, best exemplified by the hospice movement, as pioneered by Dame Cecily Saunders. Here they do follow the way of Wisdom by bringing together spiritual, moral and physical aspects of health as we see focused in Proverbs 3:7: 'Do not be wise in your own eyes; fear the LORD, shun evil. This will bring health to your body and nourishment to your bones.' Instead of rushing the terminally ill off the stage of life by killing them, the hospice movement specializes in treating the person as a whole, as someone loved and valued, using counselling to work through emotional concerns,

Christian ministers to attend to spiritual needs, careful use of pain-relieving analgesics so that there is a dignified, gradual letting go. Instead of dying lonely, frightened and bewildered, there is a quiet, confident, caring passage from this world to the next. As Dame Cecily Saunders would often say to her patients, 'You matter because you are you, and we will not only enable you to die with dignity, but to live until you die.'

Which approach captures more the spirit of Wisdom and the spirit of Christ: Dr. Kevorkian with his suicide machine or Dr. Saunders and her hospice? Who would you rather have treating you?

6

'The best days of your life?' An education for life

Proverbs 4:1-9

[1] Listen, my sons, to a father's instruction;
    pay attention and gain understanding.
[2] I give you sound learning,
    so do not forsake my teaching.
[3] When I was a boy in my father's house,
    still tender, and an only child of my mother,
[4] he taught me and said,
    'Lay hold of my words with all your heart;
    keep my commands and you will live.
[5] Get wisdom, get understanding;
    do not forget my words or swerve from them.
[6] Do not forsake wisdom, and she will protect you;
    love her, and she will watch over you.
[7] Wisdom is supreme; therefore get wisdom.
    Though it cost all you have, get understanding.
[8] Esteem her, and she will exalt you;
    embrace her, and she will honour you.
[9] She will set a garland of grace on your head
    and present you with a crown of splendour.'

Proverbs 22:6

Train a child in the way he should go,
    and when he is old he will not turn from it.

Proverbs 13:24

He who spares the rod hates his son,
    but he who loves him is careful to discipline him.

Proverbs 3:11

My son, do not despise the LORD's discipline
    and do not resent his rebuke.

Proverbs 22:15

Folly is bound up in the heart of a child,
    but the rod of discipline will drive it far from him.

Nine year old James hadn't done too well in the geography test the day before and he knew it. So, he thought that he might as well draw on what he had learnt at Sunday school and decided to pray about it. That evening, he knelt beside his bed and prayed: 'Dear God, please make Sydney the capital of New Zealand.'

There is one boy who not only needed to improve his education in geography but in theology as well! We have to admit that concern for education is almost becoming a national obsession. Throughout the major part of the 1980s and 90s, standards in education occupied a central place in national politics. Tony Blair, for instance, declared, 'Our one priority is education, education, education.' All of this reflects a genuine concern that many people have in wanting the best education for their children.

It seems that at the political level there are at least two arguments at work which constitute the main driving force for improving educational standards. The first is a pragmatic one. If Britain is to compete in the world market then it must have an educated workforce, we cannot trail behind our competitors. The second is more of a social concern. The moral fabric of our society is deteriorating. Each year we have around five million reported crimes in this country compared to under 300,000 before the Second World War. With the accompanying dissolution of the basic building block of society – the family – many are now looking to schools to fill the moral vacuum, much to the despair of teaching staff. A few years ago, the General Secretary of the National Association of Schoolmasters/Union of Women Teachers, Nigel de Gruchy, said: 'We are having cases brought to us of nursery-age children totally beyond our control at three or four years of age. Violence and disruption have spread rapidly down the age group in the last decade.' That is what our primary school teachers are now having to face. However, it is highly questionable whether as a society we can expect to pass the buck so readily on to our schools to do the job that parents ought to be doing.

In turning to the Book of Proverbs in order to see how Wisdom views education, we discover that something far more radical is required than any politician has yet suggested if we are going to see an upturn in our children's educational well-being.

Education in Proverbs is seen to be primarily the responsibility of the *parent*. 'When I was a boy in my father's house, still tender, and an only child of my mother, *he* taught me and said, "Lay hold of my words with all your heart"' (4:3-4). It is also the task of the mother to impart instruction to her children: 'Listen, my son, to your father's instruction and do not forsake your *mother's* teaching' (1:8). In the sort of culture in which

Jesus was brought up it was expected that the father of the household would be the main teacher, teaching his sons his trade. But there was also special instruction beyond the home as well as in it, mainly in synagogue schools to learn from the Law of Moses. All of this was with a specific purpose in mind. As one writer puts it, 'Jewish Education aimed not just to develop knowledge or even understanding, but knowledge and understanding applied to *daily living.*'[1] Education was about life, life as it was meant to be lived under God, and the home was viewed as the primary educational sphere of influence on the child.

The influence of the home for good or ill should not be underestimated. This point has been well made by Don Carson who argues that there is little room for optimism in improving educational standards in American schools because of the lack of support in the home. So he writes:

'In many parts of the country, if you call together any group of elementary school teachers who are Christians, you will find them troubled by what children in grades 4 and 5, or even 2 or 3, are watching on television or in the cinemas. Most of them have seen R-rated movies, usually with their parents; some have even see X-rated films, usually as videos, at home. Many of the same parents, who are terribly

1. William Strange, *Children in the Early Church*, Paternoster, 1996, p.13.

concerned that schools do not manipulate their children in the moral arena and are pulling for their children to make good grades, have simply not thought through these incongruities. One does not generate responsible citizens with values – clarification at school; equally, one does not generate responsible citizens by extolling morally unfounded virtues at school, while having them flouted in the home. If greed, cheating on taxes, broken marriages, self-centredness, and promiscuity are not opposed at home and displaced by the corresponding opposite virtues of generosity, integrity, fidelity, self-denial, and purity, institutional changes will matter fairly little.'[2]

The plain fact remains that the home still constitutes the formative stage in developing a child's character and the Bible recognises that.

So let us follow through some of the main strands in Proverbs to see what it has to say about the goal of education, the basis for education, and the means of education.

The goal of education
First of all what is the educative goal?

In order to measure success you have to have a pretty clear idea of what it is you are aiming at. The impression being gained today is that a successful education offered by a school is gauged solely by the SATS (Standard Attainment Targets) scores or where they appear in the league tables,

---

D. A. Carson, *The Gagging of God*, IVP, 1996, p.396.

which is hardly noble. The way of wisdom, however, would rate education differently, mainly in terms of *character formation*. That is, a person is said to be educated not by the quantity of information they have absorbed but by the quality of life they are living. Proverbs is not just concerned with producing tadpole-like children, small bodies and big heads, but well-rounded individuals. So words like love, faithfulness, righteousness, discernment, truthful-ness, litter the pages of Proverbs. Acquiring a moral repertoire, as well as understanding nature and the workings of the world, is seen as integral to a wholesome education. Indeed it is true that 'Wise men store up knowledge' (10:14), but also 'The truly righteous man attains life' (11:19). Being a good student means being a good person; the two are more or less synonymous.

Throughout the 1960s, 70s and 80s the trend in the West was to avoid being specific about moral content, so non-directive approaches dominated, which involved never telling a child what they should or shouldn't do, but helping them find their own way forward, whichever direction that might happen to be. The result can be summed up in the words of one student who described his course in ethics by saying, 'I learned there was no such thing as right or wrong, just good and bad arguments.'

Let me relate what has happened in a little town

in Texas called Tyler. The whole population has joined together to promote what they call 'character education'. Schools choose a value of the month to promote. When police officers in their squad cars see children doing a good deed, they turn on their sirens and award the children with a certificate. This began four years ago and surprise, surprise, the number of children fighting in school or being expelled has dropped significantly. But note the key – *all* the people – parents, politicians, police, teachers were behind it. In other words there was a moral consensus at work. They were in effect carrying out Proverbs 22:6: 'Train a child in the way he *should* go, and when he is old he will not turn from it.'

The basis for education

This leads us to ask: what is the basis for a lasting education? Proverbs leaves us in no doubt about the answer to that question and it comes right at the beginning: 'The fear of the LORD is the beginning of knowledge' (1:7); 'Trust in the LORD with all your heart and lean not on your own understanding; in all your ways acknowledge him and he will make your paths straight' (3:5). Wisdom is all a matter of viewing the world God's way, with God's revelation providing the necessary framework which alone makes sense of life, giving it some sort of coherence and direction. This is sometimes called a world view, a kind of moral map with the main points located so we can steer our way through life to maximum benefit. Accordingly, whatever it is that is to be studied, whether science, history, or home economics, all of these things can be placed within a Christian framework, in terms of the Creator-Redeeming God, and where they can be made sense of.

However, over the last 100 years or so our society has been marching to quite a different tune, what is referred to as secularism. Secularisation is the process whereby God and religion are pushed to the margins of life and so make no significant contribution at all to the policies and values adopted by society. By and large, politics and education carry on as if God were not there. And it is this secular view of things which has dominated education theory.

Without doubt, the man who more than any other has shaped the way we teach in schools in the West is the eighteenth-century thinker Jean Jacques Rousseau. Put simply, he argued that at heart children are innately good. The problem, he maintained, was the surroundings and especially the imposition of moral constraints by society. He put his ideas down in an essay called 'The Social Contract' with its famous opening line, 'Man is born free and everywhere he is in chains'. He saw the real tyranny to freedom (that is, freedom from personal obligations – autonomy) to be the family, church and state. Furthermore in his book *Emile* he showed how little children should be free to follow their own instincts – non-directive education. Let them be free to express themselves, explore for themselves, find out not by rote learning but by enquiring experimentation.

Let me fill out the picture a little more of this doyen of modern educational theory.

Rousseau was a drifter, drifting from job to job and mistress to mistress. So little wonder he was keen on promoting permissiveness, he had a personal agenda. Eventually he ended up living with a servant girl called Therese. When she presented him with a baby he was, to use his own words, 'thrown into the greatest embarrassment'. His ambition, you see, was to be accepted into the high class of Parisian society, and an illegitimate baby would likely scotch his chances of success. The result was that a few days later, a tiny blanketed bundle was left on the doorstep of the local orphanage. Over the years, four more children from Rousseau and Therese appeared on that doorstep. Historical records show that most babies in that orphanage died. The few that survived roamed the streets as beggars. Rousseau put his own children there knowing full well this was the case. What is more, he had the audacity to defend his callous actions by saying he could not do his important academic work, which involved writing educational theory, in a house 'filled with domestic cares and the noise of children'. And this is the man who would tell us how our children should be raised!

Because there is no unifying world view in our society, education has become fragmented – we have a list of subjects which do not seem to bear any relation to each other. Understandably, as a result, young people are asking, 'What is the point? Why should I study the Battle of Waterloo, it is not going to help me get a job? Life as a whole has little meaning, except to go out and enjoy yourself – so what is the point in education?' Good question, and as far as the secularist is concerned impossible to answer in any satisfactory way. Why, even teachers must find themselves wondering 'Why am I teaching this?' And trying to get good exam results so that they provide a meal ticket to a better job cannot be sufficient motivation for any thinking person. Neither is it enough to try and get children to treat each other with respect, for again they can turn around and ask why? Just because teacher says so? So what? Something else is required, something much bigger and better.

What that something is was spelt out a few years ago by David Klinghoffer in an article in the *Wall Street Journal*: 'A person doesn't accept a new, rigorous system of moral action because it might in the long run prop up civilized society.' A person submits to a demanding moral system 'because he believes it is the will of God'. Exactly! The 'fear of the Lord.'

Wisdom argues that as far as experience is concerned, God's ways are the best ways, for they fit in with the way God has made us and the world. What we believe matters. If it is taught implicitly that there are no moral absolutes, that all is relative, then this will eventually filter out into society when the children get older. If happiness is the supreme value, then if someone gets happiness by going out on a drunken rampage, who are we to object? If it is objected, 'we should not harm other people' and there is no God or judgement day and all that we are destined for is worm food at the end of the day, why should an individual bother about that? We need to remind ourselves and others that the motivation for education in the West came from Christianity. The founding of our universities, the pioneering Sunday schools and later church schools, came out of the belief that learning is good; it reflects something of our God-given image, enabling us to be good stewards of God's world as well as instilling us with a sense of obligation, in the words of Faraday, to 'think God's thoughts after him.' Learning was never meant to be cut loose from its moral moorings or from the greater goal in life which is to know God. Therefore, Solomon tells us that if we seek wisdom then 'you will fear the Lord and find knowledge of *God*.' Is it any wonder then that some of the most popular schools are now the ones with the clearest moral base?

The means of education

For those brought up in school before the 1960s the main method of learning would have been 'talk and chalk' – the traditional didactic method. The teacher spoke, the pupil listened and made notes. In the 1960s and 70s the emphasis became more on learning through experience – the so-called heuristic method. Instead of being told that the amount of light affects the rate a green plant produces food you got the children to carry out an experiment to find out for themselves.

Interestingly enough, in Proverbs we discover that *both* methods are encouraged. We find that in chapters 1–9 there is the repeated refrain 'Listen, my son to a father's instructions; do not forget my teaching' – memorise. This is especially so when the children are young. In chapters 10–31 the focus is on learning from experience, observing what happens and drawing the appropriate conclusions. Isn't it striking to see how contemporary the Bible is!

But there is another aspect integral to education and that is 'discipline'; in fact the word 'discipline' in Proverbs can be translated 'education'. 'He who heeds discipline shows the way to life' (10:17). 'He who spares the rod hates his son, but he who loves him is careful to discipline him' (13:24).

Corporal punishment is seen in the Scriptures as a necessary part of the education of the young. Why? For one thing it is following the method of the greatest teacher of all – God: 'My son, do not despise the LORD's discipline... because he disciplines those he loves' (3:11).

But also it is being true to human nature. In spite of what Rousseau taught, children are not pure little souls who are only corrupted by society and if left to get on by themselves they would grow up as angels. William Golding's *Lord of the Flies* illustrates graphically what happens to children if left to themselves – they grow up as savages. Back in 1965, referring to his classic work, Golding wrote:

> 'I believed then that man was sick – not exceptional man but average man. I believed that the condition of man was to be a morally diseased creature. To many of you this will seem trite, obvious and familiar in theological terms. Man is a fallen being, he is gripped by original sin. His nature is sinful and his state is perilous. I accept the theology and admit the triteness; but what is trite is true.'

The Bible teaches original sin: 'Folly is *bound up* in the heart of a child, but the rod of discipline will drive it far from him' (22:15). Because of natural, moral corruption, children are inclined to selfishness, cheating, bullying and being spiteful. Punishment is meant to make them less inclined to satisfying these fallen tendencies. They are to learn that it hurts to do wrong and is rewarding to do right. Education in itself without moral correction does little except to produce *clever* sinners. I know it is not fashionable or 'PC' to speak of corporal punishment, but that is often because of exaggerated pictures of abuse portrayed by the anti-smacking lobby. But wisdom is insistent: 'Do not withhold discipline from a child; if you punish him with the rod he will not die. Punish him with the rod and save his *soul* from death' (23:13). How many children's souls have been all but ruined by a failure to do this very thing? But again note the context of corporal punishment. Primarily it is to be administered by a loving parent; that element can be absent in schools and so all the more difficult to take by the pupil, let alone administer by the teacher. But if the parents agree and the teachers act in *loco parentis*, then with the appropriate checks and balances our schools could do a lot worse than have such sanctions in place.

Perhaps we ought to take stock and ask: what sort of education are we giving our children? At home do we pray with them, read the Bible with them, discuss with them what they have seen on TV from a Christian point of view? Do we discipline them, lovingly shaping their character? Are we taking an active interest in the school they attend? As a church, are we praying for Christian teachers? – they certainly need it and would welcome it.

John Milton captures the spirit of wisdom well when he writes: 'The End, then, of learning is to repair the ruins of our first parents by regaining to know God aright, and out of that knowledge to love him, to be like him, as we may the nearest, by possessing our souls of true virtue, which, being united to the heavenly grace of faith, makes up the highest perfection.'

7

The Problem of
Self-worth
Psalm 8

Psalm 8

[1]O Lord, our Lord,
    how majestic is your name in all the earth!

You have set your glory
    above the heavens.
[2]From the lips of children and infants
    you have ordained praise
because of your enemies,
    to silence the foe and the avenger.

[3]When I consider your heavens,
    the work of your fingers,
the moon and the stars,
    which you have set in place,
[4]what is man that your are mindful of him,
    the son of man that you care for him?
[5]You have made him a little lower than the heavenly
        beings
    and crowned him with glory and honor.

[6]You made him ruler over the works of your hands;
    you put everything under his feet:
[7]all flocks and herds,
    and the beasts of the field,
[8]the birds of the air,
    and the fish of the sea,
    all that swim the paths of the seas.

[9]O Lord, our Lord,
    how majestic is your name in all the earth!

She was in her late teens, hair dyed shocking red, nose pierced and studded – a punk. When asked about her beliefs and sense of value, this is how she replied: 'I belong to the Blank Generation, I have no beliefs, I belong to no community, tradition or anything like that. I'm lost in this vast, vast world. I belong nowhere, I have absolutely no identity.' This loss of meaning and significance is one which is not solely restricted to the young, many older people, too, feel that same aching inner void. The American comedian and film maker Woody Allen, now in his sixties, says that once religion is abandoned all we are left with is 'Alienation, loneliness and emptiness verging on madness'. In his film *Annie Hall* we have the classic comment that life is divided into 'the horrible and the miserable' – that's all there is. Therefore, given such sentiments as these, which are typical of many, we perhaps should not be so surprised to discover that a low self-esteem is quite common today.

The roots of the problem
Sometimes the origin of such a negative self-image lies in an emotionally deprived childhood, one starved of love and affection. Maybe it stems from a more recent tragedy of unrequited love or perhaps having been abandoned for someone else, which is devastating. But I would suspect that it is simply the cultural atmosphere we breathe

which makes belief that we are of value difficult to maintain with any conviction; after all, if the universe is a result of one cosmic accident, then we too are accidents, and the funny thing about accidents is that, like spilt milk, they are not significant, they are quite meaningless. So little wonder that many people today feel worthless nonentities. It is tragic.

But there has been an over-reaction to this as seen in the popular 'human potential' movement in counselling. Here the watchword is 'self-fulfilment'. So psychotherapeutic books about getting in touch with yourself or, as Maslow calls it, 'self-actualization' are selling like hot cakes. An advertisement appeared in *Psychology Today* which summarised the essence of this outlook: 'I love me, I am not conceited, I'm just a good friend to myself. And I like to do whatever makes me feel good.'

Some Christians too have been drawn into this movement of self-love based on a misunderstanding of the command given by Moses and endorsed by Jesus that we are to 'love our neighbour as ourselves'. The argument goes that in order to love our neighbours as ourselves, we must, as a matter of right and logic, begin by loving ourselves. But this is to totally miss the point being made by the commandment. The underlying assumption of this imperative is that we *do* love ourselves. It is, therefore, like the golden rule of 'do to others what you would have them do to you'; we know how we like to be treated and how we don't like being treated, so this provides us with a rough and ready guide on how to treat others, namely, to love as we would want to be loved. But in the Bible, *self*-love as such is seen to be a sinful thing. After all, what is the essence of sin but that we are curved in on ourselves, placing self, rather than God, at the centre of the universe. And so Paul, in 2 Timothy 3:1-5, tells us that one of the hallmarks of the last days is that people will be 'lovers of themselves' instead of 'lovers of God,' and that is precisely where we are in our society today.

Indeed self-love is itself a major contributory factor to the problem of self-worth. One Christian thinker who analysed the chaos caused by self-love was Blase Pascal in his *Pensees*:

'The essence of self-love is to love only oneself; to be interested for nothing but oneself. But what is gained by this? A man cannot prevent this object of his love being full of defects and miseries; he wishes to be great, and sees himself to be little; he wishes to be happy, and feels himself miserable; he wishes to be perfect, and sees himself full of imperfections; he wishes to be an object of the esteem and love of his fellow men, and sees that his faults deserve their aversion and condemnation. This embarrassment produces the most unjust and criminal passion imaginable; for he conceives a mortal hatred against that truth which forces him to behold and condemn his faults; he wishes it were annihilated, and unable to destroy it in its essence, he endeavours to destroy his own apprehension, and that of others; that is, he employs his utmost efforts to conceal his defects, both from himself and others, and cannot bear that men should point them out to him, or even see them. Certainly to be full of defects is an evil; but it is a much greater evil, if we are full of them, to be unwilling to know the fact; since this is adding a voluntary illusion to their number.... What a chimera is a man; what a novelty; what a chaos; what a compound of inconsistencies; a judge of all things, yet a feeble earthworm; a depository of truth, yet a heap of uncertainty; the glory and the outcast of the universe.'[1]

The problem of low self-worth at root is really a problem of wrong thinking about ourselves. Just how are we to view ourselves properly? How can we renounce the two extremes of self-hatred on the one hand and self-love on the other, neither despising nor flattering ourselves? The answer is to go back and observe what the Bible teaches and embrace its wisdom. As we do so, we discover a portrait of human beings which is neither pessimistic nor optimistic, but realistic. The biblical picture of men and women is that we are a bundle of contradictions – there is so much about us which is glorious and noble and so much that is shameful and debasing. The same mind which

1. Blase Pascal, *Thoughts on Religion and Philosophy*, John Grant, translation by I. Taylor, 1894, pp.9, 10, 46.

can design a rocket to put men on the moon is the same mind that can design killing machines to wipe out men on the earth. Again, Pascal's observations are apposite on this point:

'I blame equally those who make it their sole business to extol man and those who take on them to blame him, and those also who attempt to amuse him. I can approve none but those who examine his nature with sorrow and compassion. It is dangerous to show man in how many respects he resembles the lower animals, without pointing out his grandeur. It is also dangerous to direct his attention to his grandeur without keeping him aware of his degradation. It is still more dangerous to leave him ignorant of both; but to exhibit both to him will be most beneficial.'[2]

That is what we are, a Jekyll and Hyde – a combination of the Good, the Bad and the Ugly.

God's eye view on the matter
So let us in part take stock of how God sees us, which of course means finding out how the Lord Jesus sees us. And when we turn to him we discover two things: first, he enables us to engage in self-respect; second, he calls us to self-denial.

Being positive
From one point of view Jesus encourages a very positive attitude towards other human beings and

2. *Ibid.*, p. 6.

indeed ourselves. There is the occasion in the Sermon on the Mount when he said, 'Stop worrying,' stop fretting about what you are going to eat, what you are going to drink, what sort of clothes you are going to wear – and he points to some of the birds hovering around their nests, feeding titbits to their young, and says, 'Look, your heavenly Father feeds them, are you not much more valuable than they?' (Matt. 6:25-34). Jesus here is employing what is known as an *a fortiori* argument, moving from the lesser to the greater, expecting the answer to be a resounding 'yes, – we are of infinite value'. And why did Jesus say that? Because Jesus believed the Old Testament. He held the view of Genesis that men and women are the jewel in the crown of God's creation – that of all the beings in the universe only men and women are God-like, bearing his image (Gen. 1:26-27). He would have endorsed wholeheartedly the sentiment of the Psalmist as he stood beneath the night sky overawed by the vastness of space, the darkness which was only broken by the stars strewn like diamonds across a gigantic black velvet cloth. And pondering the immensity of it all exclaims, 'What is man that you, Almighty God, are mindful of him, or the son of man that you should care for him?' Indeed, what are we compared to the grandeur of the cosmos? He tells us, 'You have made him a little lower than the angels and crowned him with glory and honour.'

That is what we are, a millimetre down from these amazing ministering spirits that fly at God's bidding – the angels. But while these creatures are simply God's messengers we are God's managers, for the Psalmist goes on to say: 'You made him ruler over the works of your hands; you put everything under his feet.' Our status in God's creation is second to none. Several years ago a young black American boy, rebelling against the inferiority feelings inculcated into him by whites, put up a banner in his room and on it was written, 'I'm me and I'm good, 'cos God don't make no junk.' The grammar may be bad but the theology is spot on! You bet he doesn't make junk – he makes each individual unique, of supreme value to him, everyone personally known to him by name. Jesus in his teaching endorsed the Old Testament view that we do matter to God.

Modelling self-worth

Jesus did not only *teach* this, he exemplified it in the way he treated people. One cannot help but be amazed, as one reads the Gospels, at how Jesus despised nobody and disowned nobody. On the contrary he actually went out of his way to make friends with those whom everyone else had written off as beyond the pale. So he spoke courteously to women in public, an unheard of thing for men to do in those days. He welcomed children in a culture where they were hardly seen, let alone heard. Samaritans, religious mongrels as far as any self-respecting Jew was concerned, were the objects of Jesus' love. He allowed those with leprosy to approach him, when to others their idea of care in the community amounted to long-term isolation in a leper colony – and he actually touched them. Can you imagine what that meant to them? Can you even begin to envisage living for twenty, thirty, forty years without anyone touching you, holding you, kissing you? That was the lot of these poor people, so when this man touched them, let alone healed them, the sense of acceptance and worth must have been overwhelming to the point of tears. Whether they were rich or poor, religious or pagan, sick or healthy, it didn't matter; every single person was valued and loved by him, and by loving them he actually increased their value.

But it is the death of Christ which spells out more clearly than anything else the great value Jesus placed upon people, that he was determined to suffer and die for them. He was the Good Shepherd who came into the hostile desert of this world to seek out and save the one lost sheep (John 10; Luke 15:3ff). Indeed, he laid down his life for his sheep (John 10:15). As Archbishop William Temple expressed it: 'My worth is what I am worth to God; and that is a marvellous great deal, for Christ died for me. Thus, incidentally, what gives to each of us his highest worth gives the same worth to everyone; in all that matters most are we equal.'[3] This is the way Paul puts it in Galatians 2:20: 'The Son of God, who loved me and gave himself for me' – the very one who had previously sought to destroy the church, who had cursed Jesus day and night – God's Son died for him! That is the measure of God's love, that is the value *he* places on us. As Martin Luther said, 'God doesn't love us because of our worth, we are of worth because God loves us.'

The flip side of the coin

But this has to be balanced by the other side of our nature which Jesus saw only too clearly – the fact that we are morally corrupted. Though made in God's image, that image has been defaced by our sin. Indeed, it is in this morally imperfect state, inclined towards wrong and biased against God, that we are born into the world – as David said in Psalm 51, 'In sin did my mother conceive me.' Jesus too shared this Old Testament view of human nature as hopelessly flawed: 'Out of men's hearts come evil thoughts, sexual immorality, theft, murder, adultery, greed, malice, deceit, lewdness, envy, slander, arrogance and folly' (Mark 7:21-23). I can check every single one of those off in my heart in some measure, and they

---

3. William Temple, *The Citizen and Churchman*, Eyre and Spottiswood, 1951, p.74.

115

are there in your hearts too. Like a beautiful portrait that has been defaced, that is what we are. And it is this aspect of ourselves that, far from loving, we are to deny.

Our self is a complex mixture of good and evil, dignity and shame. The self we are to turn from is the fallen self, the corrupted self which would promote self-love at the expense of loving others. So we must say no to our greed, no to our desire for sex outside marriage, no to taking advantage of the less well-off in order to feather our own nests. The self we are to affirm and respect is our created self, everything within us that is compatible with Jesus Christ, such as our sense of doing right, of upholding family life, our stewardship of God's earth and the like.

Be patient, God isn't finished with me yet
But Christians aren't just created and fallen human beings, they are redeemed human beings, in the process of being recreated by God's Spirit. As they put their trust in Jesus Christ who died for their sins on the cross they become reborn spiritually (Tit. 3:5). God's Holy Spirit starts remaking them, clearing away the moral rubbish and instilling into them a new set of values as they read his Word, the Bible. He also introduces us to God as our heavenly Father and to other Christians as brothers and sisters. Indeed, we become stamped with the very character of Christ, being made increasingly

116

into his likeness – so the deformed image starts to be reformed (Col. 3:10). In other words, Christians are given a power so that they can start saying no to self and yes to God. What is more, they are given a new status they never had before, the status of being God's children (1 John 5:1).

I really do adore children, I think they are great. But I have a special love for my own three children – not because they are cleverer or better or more handsome than other people's children, but simply because they are *my* children. As such they have a unique value in my sight and I love them beyond anything words could ever express. And the Bible teaches the same about Christians and the heavenly Father. Because by God's grace we are members of *his* family, the Church, there is a special status we have in his eyes simply because we are *his* children. According to the apostle Paul in Galatians 4 we have been adopted into God's family by his Spirit – so that we now possess full rights as members of the divine family, which means that God now looks upon us with the same love and affection he looks upon Jesus. Isn't that a marvellous thought? When God contemplates you as a Christian (which he does by the way night and day – you are never out of his thoughts for a single moment), he contemplates you as he would his eternal Son, with all the love and devotion and passion he has for Christ ('Let the world know that you sent me and have loved them even as you have loved me', John 17:23). And one day in the fullness of time he is going to welcome us into his eternal kingdom, and then we are going to have the surprise of our lives for, to our utter astonishment, we will discover that we are like a perfectly polished mirror, reflecting the beauty and wholesome character of the Lord Jesus himself: 'We know that when he (Jesus) appears we shall be like him' (1 John 3:2). The gentleness which characterises him will characterise us, the self-giving love which radiates from him will radiate from us, the passion for holiness and all that is good which marks him will also mark us. That is the destiny of a Christian believer. How does one's sense of self-worth rate after contemplating that?

Here are some wise words of the Christian counsellor Larry Crabb who tackles this question of people's need to feel worthwhile which he argues is related to two other basic needs, the need for significance and security:[4]

> 'I will come to feel significant as I have an eternal impact on people around me by ministering to them. If I fail in business, if my wife leaves me, if my church roll drops, I can still enjoy the thrilling significance of belonging to the Ruler of the universe who has a job for me to do. My need for security demands that I be unconditionally loved, accepted and cared for, now

---

4. Larry Crabb, *Effective Bible Counselling*, Marshalls, 1985, p. 65

and for ever. God has seen me at my worst and still loved me to the point of giving his life for me. That kind of love I can never lose.'

That kind of love and the significance it occasions can only be found in Christ. And it is precisely that kind of love and significance he offers to any who will humbly receive it.

8

If Only I Had
The Time
Psalm 90

Psalm 90

¹Lord, you have been our dwelling place
    throughout all generations.
²Before the mountains were born
    or you brought forth the earth and the world,
    from everlasting to everlasting you are God.
³You turn men back to dust,
    saying, 'Return to dust, O sons of men.'
⁴For a thousand years in your sight
    are like a day that has just gone by,
    or like a watch in the night.
⁵You sweep men away in the sleep of death;
    they are like the new grass of the morning –
⁶though in the morning it springs up new,
    by evening it is dry and withered.

⁷We are consumed by your anger
    and terrified by your indignation.
⁸You have set our iniquities before you,
    our secret sins in the light of your presence.
⁹All our days pass away under your wrath;
    we finish our years with a moan.
¹⁰The length of our days is seventy years –
    or eighty, if we have the strength;
yet their span is but trouble and sorrow,
    for they quickly pass, and we fly away.

[11]Who knows the power of your anger?
   For your wrath is as great as the fear that is due
      to you.
[12]Teach us to number our days aright,
   that we may gain a heart of wisdom.

[13]Relent, O LORD! How long will it be?
   Have compassion on your servants.
[14]Satisfy us in the morning with your unfailing love,
   that we may sing for joy and be glad all our days.
[15]Make us glad for as many days as you have afflicted
      us,
   for as many years as we have seen trouble.
[16]May your deeds be shown to your servants
   your splendour to their children.

[17]May the favour of the Lord our God rest upon us;
   establish the work of our hands for us –
   yes, establish the work of our hands.

Meet Mr. Modern. He is digitilized, schedulised and highly organised. Time means money. Mr. Modern wastes no time, he refuses to give way to the trivial at the expense of the weighty, and the important is *never* to be sacrificed on the altar of the urgent. His filofax rules with relentless authority. Mr. Modern lives life in the fast lane, lunch is for wimps, time means money; more money to spend on more leisure, but there seems so little time for leisure. Mr. Modern is important, indispensable, he can be paged anywhere at anytime – Mr. Modern has a mobile phone, now he can make more of the time as he sits in the interminable traffic jam; more business, more money – time means money. A moment of quiet intrudes into Mr. Modern's precious time as his mind wanders for a moment and settles on those two little figures left lying in bed. How old were they now? Five and six, or was it eight and nine? Goodness, how time flies! He must, simply *must*, spend more time with them. Yes, that's what he will do next year – time permitting, of course.

Although he does not know it, Mr. Modern is a victim – a victim of a new tyranny – the tyranny of time. This is the modern view of time. Time is a *commodity* to be bought and sold, an *opportunity* to be active, in business and in leisure, and the more that can be crammed into it the better. And what I can't do today, I can put off till tomorrow, the thought never occurring that there may be no tomorrow. For part of this new attitude towards time is that the future is often taken for granted, even by the old and the infirm. In the words of the musical *Fame*, people behave as if they are going to live for ever.

Although we dream of having more leisure and so fill our lives with labour-saving devices to achieve this, the pace somehow never seems to slacken. As we try to fit as much as possible into the day and squeeze the last drop of life out of each hour, we seem to suffer for it. Time, it appears, can seriously damage our health, not to mention our work, families and even our spirituality. After all, who has time for God? Although, of course, it is not time as such, but our attitude towards it that causes such modern phenomena as burnout and breakdowns.

The view of time as a commodity is quite recent, dating from the industrial revolution and the invention of accurate timepieces in the eighteenth century. With the rise of industry came the idea of *time* management, how to get twenty-six hours out of every day. But the Bible writers didn't even divide the day into twenty-four hours; it was sunset to sunset, season to season, festival to festival, year to year. Time was not something to be spent, like money; it was a gift to be cherished like love.

The modern problem

What has happened is that we have lost any sense that our lives constitute a story, a narrative, which has a beginning and an end. That what matters is what we make of our lives, how we give them shape and direction by what we are and what we do. For many today, life tends to be fragmented, with little sense of the past and little concern for the future. One of the dominant features of postmodernism is the lack of what is called a 'meta-narrative', an overall, arching story which gives meaning to what we do and who we are. The result is that we live for the 'now', the instant, filling our lives with activities like an alcoholic would fill his stomach with drink. As soon as we have done one thing we are then on to the next and before we know it, our lives are over. For you see, if there is no God, then there is no real significance to our lives, time simply becomes something to be filled and got through.

The havoc caused by this view of time to family life, for example, is well captured by the song 'The Cat's in the Cradle;' 'A child arrived the other day, he came into the world in the usual way. But there were planes to catch and bills to pay. He learnt to walk while I was away and he learnt to talk before I knew it. And as he grew he used to say 'I'm going to be like you, Dad, I'm going to be like you.' *The cat's in the cradle and the silver spoon and the little boy blew and the man in the moon*. When are you coming home Dad? I don't know when, but we'll get together then son, we'll have a good time then. My son turned ten the other day, he said thanks for the ball, Dad, let's play. I said not today son, I've got lots to do. He said that's OK and he walked away, and his smile never dimmed, it said 'I'm gonna be like him, I'm gonna be like him. *The cat's in the cradle and the silver spoon and the little boy blew and the man in the moon.* Well, he came home from college the other day so much like a man that I just had to say 'I'm proud of you son. Can you sit for a while?' He said, 'I'm sorry Dad,' and said with a smile, 'what I'd really like is to borrow the car keys, could I have them please?' When are you coming home son? I don't know when, but we'll get together then, we'll have a good time then. I've long since retired and my son moved away. I called him up the other day, I'd like to see you son if you don't mind. He said, 'I'd love to Dad if I could find the time, but the new job's a hassle and the kids have got the flu, but its been nice talking to you, Dad, it's been nice talking to you. And as he hung up the phone it occurred to me, he'd grown up just like me.'

Back to the Bible

How we view time has far-reaching practical consequences, for good or for ill, for our lives as individuals, as a society and as a church.

How, then, according to the Scriptures should we think of time and have our lives shaped accordingly? Insight into what the answers might be are afforded by the wisdom contained in Psalm 90.

The timeless God
The first thing we are to ponder is that God is timeless: 'Before the mountains were born or you brought forth the earth and the world, from everlasting to everlasting you are God' (Psalm 90:2). What that means is simply this: that God has always been and will always be, there was never a moment when he did not exist in his glorious perfection and holiness. He is self-existent and wholly self-sufficient dependent upon no one and nothing. This is what theologians call the aseity of God (from the Latin *a se esse*, being from oneself). He does not grow old, or grow tired, or change his plans and purposes; he will never become less loving, less just, less caring. He is completely perfect within himself as Father, Son and Holy Spirit. He is untouched by time because he is not bound by time – and so he sees our time quite differently to us: 'For a thousand years in your sight are like a day that has just gone by' (v.4) – he is everlasting.

All of that, of course, stands in such stark contrast to us who are bound by time. We do grow old, change our plans, and diminish in our intellectual, physical and spiritual powers. Our youthfulness evaporates eventually. In short, we are mortal: 'You sweep men away in the sleep of death; they are like the new grass of the morning – though in the morning it springs up new, by evening it is dry and withered' (v.5).

For the Christian, time is a gift allotted to him by the everlasting God: 'The length of our days is seventy years – or eighty, if we have the strength' (v.10).

The picture the Bible paints is that there is an everlasting God from whom we come – he made us; there is a God to whom we are going – he will judge us; there is a God through whom we exist, he sustains us; and there is a God for whom we are made – he loves us. I would suggest that when Christians begin to think of their lives in that way –as coming from God, going to God, existing through God and being made for God – then their view of time and what they do with their lives will be radically different from their non-Christian neighbours.

A change of view

For a start, instead of thinking of time as a commodity we own – 'Don't take up *my* time,' we shall see it as a gracious gift which is on loan – it is God's time. And so, as Paul says in Ephesians 5:16, the Christian will seek to 'redeem the time,' making the best of every opportunity.

That is, the believer will see the succession of time as, if you like, windows of opportunity for God to achieve his purposes in the world and to see himself as contributing to those purposes as he works through us – sharing the gospel, raising a family, doing an honest day's work, paid or unpaid. This is what Ephesians 5:16-20 actually says:

'Be very careful, then, how you live, not as unwise but wise, making the most of every opportunity (lit. redeeming the time) because the days are evil. Therefore do not be foolish, but understand what the Lord's will is. Do not get drunk on wine, which leads to debauchery. Instead, be filled with the Spirit. Speak to one another with psalms, hymns and spiritual songs. Sing and make music in your heart to the Lord, always giving thanks to God the Father for everything, in the name of Jesus Christ.'

In other words, fools squander this gift in directionless and selfish waste, like getting drunk, what a useless activity that is and yet how common it is. The writer and broadcaster Clive James conducted an interview with the actor Mel Gibson who made this very point. Gibson, looking back on his 'hell-raising' younger days when he would drink heavily and do the most outrageous things, lamented that nothing is so wasteful as getting drunk.

Likewise, the apostle Paul, earlier on in chapter 4, gives a whole list of things which characterise a waste of time and so a waste of a life: stealing, lying, fornicating, backbiting, dirty story telling, greed. These contribute nothing constructive, they demean others and they corrupt ourselves; and at the end of their lives that is the story such folk will have written and which will be presented to God. Is that what we want? Stop squandering God's gift in this way, says Paul, instead be filled with the Spirit. What characterises that? He tells us.

Horizontally, in our relationships with each other, it means we should build each other up with the beautiful truths of God – singing psalms, spiritual songs – ministering to one another. That is such a productive use of time for that is, in part, what we were created for. Not squandering God's gifts selfishly, but sharing God's gifts lovingly. Therefore, instead of taking that window of opportunity to gossip, use it to praise. Instead of yet another night of telly watching, why not feed your mind in Bible study?

Vertically, we are to give thanks to God – that is a great use of time, for, when you think about it, that is how we will spend most of eternity immersed in heart-felt, joyful, loving praise to so glorious a Saviour. This doesn't mean we have to have praise tapes playing while we go about the housework or mending the car! But rather that we are conscious that whatever we are engaged in, it is under the loving and ever watchful eye of our Creator, knowing we are accountable to him for how we have lived our lives.

Take a break

Secondly, it means that we should take time out.

God has built in a natural rhythm into this world revolving around the figure seven. It is interesting that both after the French revolution and the Russian revolution, when they abolished the seven-day week and replaced it with a ten-day week, both societies practically collapsed – people could not cope. It's not surprising really. God has given us a seven day week which includes a Sabbath day – which means a rest day; a day which should be different from any other day, not to be crammed with meaningless activities, so becoming more work, but a day for difference, a day to meet with fellow believers, a day to meet with God in a focused way, a day, if we can, to be with family or friends, or a day just to be quiet and alone.

Have you ever been struck at how Jesus, in the midst of the most demanding ministry, would suddenly dismiss the crowd and withdraw for prayer? He would, as the RSV puts it, 'come apart with his disciples'. Here is the Son of God, who in less than three years achieved far more than kings and generals had ever achieved in a thousand years, taking time out. Why? Well, he knew his needs and limitations – even he couldn't work twenty-four hours a day seven days a week – and neither can we. But also he could have the confidence to do this because of his quiet, serene knowledge that his time was in his Father's hands, that he wasn't going to change the world by one endless round of activity, but by doing things in God's time in God's way (this is brought out especially in John's Gospel, cf. 2:4; 7:6; 11:9). And we, too, desperately need to learn this lesson. As someone once said, 'If we do not come apart, we come – apart.' Do you take time just to be quiet, to take that walk for no apparent purpose except to do it?

How time flies!
Thirdly, to know that God is timeless and we are moving towards meeting him will impress upon us how rapidly time passes: 'they quickly pass, and we fly away' (v.10). I remember when I was seventeen discussing with some school friends what it must be like being twenty-one. We couldn't imagine what it would be like reaching such a great age. Well, twenty-one came pretty quickly, as did thirty-one and forty-one and fifty-one. Eventually, you get to that age, so my older colleagues tell me, when you go to the chiropodist to get your feet fixed and you see a few of your old friends, the last thing you should do is ask 'Where is so and so?' without first checking the obituary column, because otherwise it's embarrassed looks all round! But that is where we are all heading.

Try this little thought experiment with me.

Consider the 'time line' below.

Birth ---------------------------------------Death
Where are You?

The beginning of that line is your birth, the end of that line your death. Try and take a guess at an age for the end of that line, how long you think you might live, perhaps sixty, seventy, eighty years. Now, pinpoint on that line between your birth and your death where you are at the moment. Then ask yourself: How do I feel about that? What might you do with what you have left?

That is why the psalmist says in verse 12: 'Teach us to number our days aright, that we may gain a heart of wisdom.' That is, 'Lord, teach me so to conceive time as an unrepeatable gift that I might live my life serenely with your values in mind so that my life is lived to the full.' In other words, we should live life with eternity in view.

That means if you are reading this and are not yet a Christian it is vital you become one and get right with God before it is too late. That comes through a personal one-to-one coming before God in prayer, acknowledging your need in being on the wrong side of God, believing that through his Son on the cross he has done all that is necessary to make you right with him, and asking him to come into your life by His Spirit.

But if you are a Christian, then ask God by his

Spirit to let eternity touch your life at every point. Let eternity's values set your priorities and put this world's cares into perspective. As the Lord Jesus puts it in the Sermon on the Mount: 'Seek first the kingdom of God, then all these other things shall be yours as well' (Matt. 6:33).

9

For Better for Worse.
Christian Marriage
1 Peter 3: 1-7

1 Peter 3

[1]Wives, in the same way be submissive to your husbands so that, if any of them do not believe the word, they may be won over without words by the behaviour of their wives, [2]when they see the purity and reverence of your lives. [3]Your beauty should not come from outward adornment, such as braided hair and the wearing of gold jewellery and fine clothes. [4]Instead, it should be that of your inner self, the unfading beauty of a gentle and quiet spirit, which is of great worth in God's sight. [5]For this is the way the holy women of the past who put their hope in God used to make themselves beautiful. They were submissive to their own husbands, [6]like Sarah, who obeyed Abraham and called him her master. You are her daughters if you do what is right and do not give way to fear.

[7]Husbands, in the same way be considerate as you live with your wives, and treat them with respect as the weaker partner and as heirs with you of the gracious gift of life, so that nothing will hinder your prayers.

Erica Jong is a poet, a feminist poet in fact. Shortly after she had her first baby, Ms. Jong was invited to a poetry reading before an audience of radical feminists. She decided to read several poems expressing the deep feelings she experienced in becoming a mother. She was literally booed off the stage. She was devastated. Today Erica Jong writes articles on the failure of feminism, rooted, she says, in its unwillingness to recognise the central fact in the lives of 90% of American women; the fact that they have children and that they resent being made to feel guilty about it.

There is no doubt that feminism has re-shaped the social map of Western society, some of it, it has to be willingly admitted, for the good. The blatant sexism which was prevalent in the 1960s in which I grew up as a child was rightly challenged. This was the decade when women were increasingly portrayed as exploited sex objects à la Bond or domesticated poodles as conceived in many of the sitcoms of that era. Equal opportunities was in no small measure due to the influences of feminists writers like Betty Friedan in the States and Germaine Greer in Britain. But the danger of any 'ism', whether it be feminism or chauvinism, is when what is a partial truth becomes inflated into the whole truth with damaging effects, as, when in the case of Erica Jong, motherhood is derided as unfeminine.

However, radical feminism has not just had a

negative effect on women, but on men too. Rosalin Miles in *The Independent* newspaper expresses the dilemma posed for men in this way:

> 'Over the past twenty years, feminism has been redrawing the maps, rewriting the rules and redefining the meaning of things unquestioned for thousands of years. But we have hardly given a thought to the men. And many men are left feeling like lost boys in this post-patriarchal world where their prerogatives and perks have been blown away.'

In short, there is a confusion over gender roles which is especially focused in the home.

What may come as a surprise to many of us is that similar murmurings over the role of men and women were brewing in the Roman Empire at the time Peter was writing his first letter. Indeed, there was a history of feminist revolt in ancient Rome. As early as 195 BC the matrons of Rome came out in force on to the streets in their hundreds blockading the homes of the male politicians. They were protesting against what was called the 'opium law' which restricted women's activities in the city of Rome. So powerful was their demonstration that a famous consul named Markus Porteous Cater was moved to speak to the Roman Senate in the following way: 'Romans, if every married man made sure his own wife looked up to him and respected his authority we should not have half this trouble with women in general now.... We have failed to control each woman individually and so we find ourselves quailing before a body of them.' In the centuries that followed, women became more and more vocal and belligerent. Many became involved in political intrigue, neglecting home life to such an extent that Caesar Augustus was seriously concerned with the fall in the birthrate amongst aristocratic families and sought to pass a law to rectify the situation. By the beginning of the Christian era the women of Rome were a formidable bunch and their ideas and influence extended well into other parts of the Empire.

Clarifying the context
Given this background, we should not be so surprised to find Peter writing the way he does. If through a curious blend of the legitimate liberation the Christian gospel brings in, bestowing upon women dignity in Christ, together with the political firmament of Roman feminist thinking, it may well have been that some Christian women hadn't behaved as wisely as they should have towards their husbands. Also, the husbands too needed careful instruction on how they were to treat their wives, not over-reacting to such developments with tyranny and abuse, but with consideration and respect.

But let us not think that we can dismiss what Peter says here as the reactionary words of a threatened chauvinist who simply wants to maintain the status quo. Neither militant radicalism on the one hand or knee-jerk conservatism on the other shaped Peter's view. Rather, it was shaped by God's own revelation of wisdom. What we have in these few verses is practical application of the principle stated in 2:11-12:

> I urge you as aliens and strangers in the world to abstain from sinful desires [throwing off all authority or tyrannically imposing it for instance]. Live such good lives among the pagans that, though they accuse you of doing wrong, they may see your good deeds and glorify God on the day he visits us.

Peter has already shown how this is to be worked out in two of the basic spheres of human activity where there is a distinct authority structure: the area of government (citizens and rulers) and the area of work (slaves and masters). Now he turns to a third sphere, the home and the relation between wives and husbands.

The way of wisdom

Peter addresses each member of the marriage relationship and gives a command linked to a purpose. To the wife, the command is, Be submissive. The purpose is that through their conduct their husbands might be won to the faith (v. 1). To the husband, the command is, Be considerate. The purpose is to ensure a healthy faith (v. 7).

142

In 2:13 Christian citizens are called to submit to the authority of those in government. In verse 18 it is Christian slaves who are called upon to submit to the authority of their masters. Here at the beginning of chapter 3 we have a similar submission required on the part of wives to their husbands: 'In the *same way* wives, be submissive to your husbands.' And just how that submission is to be worked out is explained in the rest of the passage.

A wise word to wives

Peter talks about 'purity', that is, chastity; so even if the wife cannot rely upon her husband's fidelity he should at least be able to rely on hers. Also he speaks of 'reverence', literally, fear (*phobos*), not a craven cowering, but showing respect, especially in public, never running the husband down. Their lives, says Peter, are to be adorned with a beauty which comes from within, identified as a 'gentle and quiet spirit' which is precious in *God's* sight. Peter calls Christians wives to behave with two audiences in mind: God and the unbelieving world, in this case, unbelieving husbands. In effect, Peter is saying to Christian wives: far from your conduct as a Christian woman being an occasion leading you to receive your husband's condemnation, it should be the very thing that prompts his commendation. As Peter puts it in verse 1, although they may not obey the word, that is the word of the gospel, they nonetheless may be won over without a word, that is by the charming lifestyle of the wife. This is something which is directly applicable to many Christian wives today who find themselves with unbelieving and, in some cases, hostile partners. Don't resent them, says Peter, as a hindrance to your faith, rather see them as an opportunity to commend your faith. Your aim must be that whenever he talks to his non-Christian friends it will be to praise you not to criticise you.

Furthermore, Christian wives are to be attractive, urges Peter in verse 3, with an attraction which doesn't come from outward adornment, such as braided hair, gold jewellery or fine clothes – the particular hallmark of the liberated Roman matrons – but that of the inner self, a beauty of spirit which does not change with the fashions of the time, nor does it fade away with age, on the contrary this beauty becomes more attractive as the years pass by. I know of very beautiful Christian women who are old in years. But this is not the result of lashings of Oil of Ulay or the trimming of the toning table but the work of God's Spirit through his Word. It is important not to misunderstand what Peter is saying at this point. He is not arguing that Christian women should look *dowdy*, for how a woman looks often does matter to a man. Rather, what matters most, or at least should do, is how the wife behaves. There is a point to this submission – winning the husband to Christ.

And just in case we are still tempted to dismiss submission to the leadership of the husband as being culturally relative, Peter draws upon Scriptural precedent: 'For this is the way the holy women of the past who put their hope in God used to make themselves beautiful. They were submissive to their own husbands, like Sarah, who obeyed Abraham and called him her master. You are her daughters if you do what is right and do not give way to fear....' (vv. 5-6).

Let me give an actual example of what Peter means.

Some years ago a young woman became a Christian. Having the zeal of a convert she let her enthusiasm get the better of her. To the chagrin of her non-Christian husband, she attended every church meeting on offer and in her idealisation of what she considered to be 'spiritual,' she paid less and less attention to her looks. The minister noticed she seemed unhappy and asked her to make an appointment to see him. She said that her unhappiness stemmed from the fact she had tried witnessing to her husband but was getting nowhere. He suggested she might want to smarten herself up a little, and try not saying anything, instead to try praying for her husband and focusing on doing things he liked doing and wait to see what happened. Several months later, the husband asked to see the minister. He said, 'Can you explain what's going on? A while ago my wife came home saying she had been born again and I didn't know what hit me. I would go to the bathroom to shave and there would be a text of Scripture stuck to the mirror. I would go to the bedroom and there would be a Bible left open on my chair with verses underlined. And she would go on and on at me to come to church. Honestly, each night it was like going to bed with Billy Graham! But then, it stopped. She seemed more content, more interested in what I was doing and in me as a person. I tell you frankly our marriage has got better. Tell me, why?' So the minister explained it to him.

A timely word to husbands

What does Peter expect husbands to do? Probably a lot more than they are doing at the moment! 'Husbands, in the same way be considerate as you live with your wives' (v.7), literally, 'live according to knowledge', or as it could be translated 'be understanding of your wives'. That is, discover what makes her tick, find out what pleases her and promote those things. And when you hit upon her dislikes, then avoid them.

From different planets?

It would seem that Peter's exhortation to 'understand' goes even deeper than that. It involves understanding the fundamental differences between men and women as God has created us, as well as taking into account the effects of the fall and acting accordingly.

A book many have found valuable in this regard is the bestseller by John Gray, *Men are from Mars and Women are from Venus*. His basic thesis is that generally men and women differ significantly in terms of motivation, needs and how they communicate and such is the difference that it's as if they come from different planets. It is only when the differences are recognised and accommodated that the two races can get along exceedingly well.

It would seem that many of our problems arise when men act as if women should be like men and women behave as if men should be like women. God has not made us so – we are to complement each other and the differences are to be acknowledged.

For example, when a wife says, 'I am tired, I can't do anything,' she doesn't want her husband to come up with a solution such as muttering from behind his newspaper, 'Why don't you cut out the shopping trip?' – which is what men have a tendency to do, be the Mr. Fix It. She is actually saying, 'I have a lot on at the moment, I want your understanding and reassurance, a hug would be great.'

By and large, women talk to relate, men talk

to inform. It then follows if men are going to relate to their wives they must talk to them and listen to them, making noises which signal they *are* listening. Women are like waves, with ups and downs, and the downs come for no apparent reason. And during those low emotional times she will be looking to the husband simply to listen and reassure her, fill her emotional tank by physical contact and *not* be given a ten-stage programme to follow on how to get her life in order. For women feelings are important, and that they are at least recognised and affirmed and not dismissed by the man as one of those feminine peculiarities is vital. That is why non-directive counselling is more successful with women than men.

Women also have a different way of evaluating actions. For a man one big act is meant to score ten points. I put up the shelf today – that should put me in credit with her for at least two weeks. It doesn't work like that. For a woman one act is worth one point. So a number of small, caring acts will be worth far more to her than the occasional big bunch of flowers. That doesn't mean that men should not get flowers, but they should try and understand how they are rated by the wife.

Women expect support without being asked and they offer it without being solicited too. Men, however, don't like to be offered advice unless they ask for it. Cross these two wires and resentment soon follows. She feels resentful because the support she expected didn't come and he feels annoyed because the advice he didn't want was given. It's a complicated business alright – but that is what 'being considerate' is all about.

What is more, this fundamental difference between the sexes which goes beyond mere physiology is underscored by Peter when he says 'treat them with respect', literally, 'preciousness', the same word he used in 2:7 where Jesus 'the stone' is described as precious to God. And why is the man to do this? Because she is the weaker partner or weaker vessel.

What does Peter mean? The context points to it referring to the wife's position within the marital structure. Relatively speaking, who is the weaker vessel in terms of authoritorial power? The King or the citizen, the master or the slave? In each case the latter. And certainly within the society to which Peter was writing there was no question at all who was the weaker in the marriage relationship – the wife. But that position, far from being taken as an opportunity to exploit the wife which the pagans may do, is by the Christian husband to be seen as an opportunity to take care of his wife, to treat her as precious.

Right at the end of verse 6 Peter recognises the tendency for some women in such marriages to be fearful, of 'giving way to fear'. Why? Because of the treatment of their husbands. Earlier

I mentioned that pagan husbands tended to exploit their position of leadership. That such criticism were only restricted to them! Christian men have to admit more than their fair share of culpability in this. So there is the Christian husband whose idea of 'headship' is little more than a thinly-veiled biblical justification for dictatorship. This is the one who without prior warning announces to his wife that he has invited friends from church around for a meal and he is sure she will come up with the goods. I am sad to say that I know of good Christian women who are but stifled shadows of what they could have been, because of the domineering activities of their Christian husbands, men who may even receive the praises of unsuspecting church members, 'Doesn't he have a model family? She seems to idolise him.' But if only they knew the fear lurking behind that front door.

That should not be. The husband's leadership in the home has more to do with responsibilities than privilege. To speak of the woman as the weaker vessel implies no inferiority of worth; on the contrary, if you have a valuable crystal vase you treat it with greater tenderness, not less. And while it may be the case that within the created order of the family the wife occupies a position of submission to the authority of her husband, when it comes to the future salvation she is a 'co-heir' with the husband.

But a final and unexpected reason is given to the husband to go out of his way to understand and care for his wife and that is the health of his faith is at stake – 'so that nothing will hinder your prayers'. Surely this is an extension of what Jesus says in the Sermon on the Mount in the context of prayer, that if we do not forgive each other God will not forgive us (Matt. 6:15). If the husband-wife relationship is impaired because of neglect, the husband-God relationship is impaired too – God will not hear his prayers. That is the measure of how seriously God expects husbands to behave properly towards their wives – they effectively get cut off from him if they don't.

Two commands of Christian wisdom which in their own respective spheres of a marriage reflect the character of Christ – wives be submissive, husbands be considerate. No wonder the early Christians were thought of as a breed apart.

10

Bring Them Up – Parenting
Ephesians 6:1-4

Ephesians 6:1-4
[1]Children, obey your parents in the Lord, for this is right. [2]'Honor your father and mother' – which is the first commandment with a promise – [3]'that it may go well with you and that you may enjoy long life on the earth.' [4]Fathers, do not exasperate your children; instead, bring them up in the training and instruction of the Lord.

A man was pushing his shopping trolley through the supermarket one day, and in it sat his little boy, screaming and lashing out at the cans on the shelves – a heap of acute embarrassment. As the red-faced parent made slow progress around the aisles, he was overheard by a lady in the same aisle saying, 'Calm down, George, it will be alright, George, be patient, George.' And suitably impressed on hearing this, she went up to the man and said, 'May I congratulate you on your calm and collected handling of the boy. And how is little George today?' To which the father replied, 'Madam, I'm George!'

I guess those of us who are parents very much identify with that man. We are George. Before we dare to give advice to others about raising children we humbly need to take stock ourselves. As a father of three that certainly applies to me. However, one of the wonderful things about being a Christian is that we are not left alone to flounder through life. We have God's book as our guide and God's Spirit as our teacher. And it is in these few verses that we strike a rich vein of wisdom regarding how we are to go about bringing up our children: 'Fathers, do not exasperate your children, instead bring them up in the training and instruction of the Lord' (Eph. 6:4). Right at the beginning of this letter, in 1:10, Paul tells us what God's plan and purpose is, to unite *all* things under the headship of Jesus Christ – and that includes, of course, the family – husbands and wives, parents and children, slaves and masters (slaves being seen as part of what we might call the 'extended family'). What is more, Christians, we are told in 5:18, are to continue being filled with the Spirit. So the question is: how should a Spirit-filled parent behave? The answer is given in Ephesians 6:4.

Although Paul here speaks directly to 'Fathers,' it is not exclusively to fathers his words apply – after all, in the previous verse mothers as well as fathers are bracketed together as those whom children are to obey, and of course there is the case of the single parent. While Paul begins with what parents should avoid doing, namely, exasperating their children, making them resentful, I want to focus on the positive command given and only in passing see how we can cause resentment to build up in our children when we depart from God's ways.

What Paul says in the original can be translated as follows: 'Fathers (and mothers) instead of goading your children so that they resent you, fondly cherish them, rearing them tenderly in the discipline and instruction of the Lord.'

Do you see how wise and balanced the Bible is? Parents are not to be harsh and cruel with their children, treating them like wild animals in need of taming, which was the view of the Romans and Greeks – rather they are to be lovingly cherished.

This is in contrast to what Plato wrote: 'Of all the wild creatures, the child is the most intractable; for insofar as it, above all others, possesses a fount of reason that is yet uncurbed, it is a treacherous, sly and most insolent creature. Wherefore a child must be strapped up, as it were, with many bridles' (Laws 808D). But neither are children to be viewed through rose-coloured spectacles as moral innocents who can be allowed to do whatever they want – the view of the eighteenth century philosopher, Rousseau; they are to be disciplined and taught 'of the Lord'.

So what does it mean to rear our children tenderly, which literally in the Greek means to 'nourish' them?

The way of love
Basic to all we do is that we show our children unconditional love.

How do we measure love for our children? The answer many will give today is in terms of the things bought for them. This was a point so well made in the Beatles song, *She's Leaving Home*. Here was a young woman who had decided to elope with her car salesman boyfriend, much to the utter bewilderment of her parents whose perplexity was expressed in the refrain, 'We gave her most of our lives, we gave her everything money could buy.' But the one thing money could not buy, and which they did not give, was love. It

157

is only too possible for a child to have the most amazing bedroom, littered with mouth-watering toys and still be the loneliest child in the world, because he or she is a stranger to unconditional love.

So what is this love? It is, in fact, a mirror of God's love for us – agape love. As Paul puts it at the beginning of chapter 5: 'Be imitators of God, therefore, as dearly loved children, and live a life of love, *just as Christ loved us and gave himself up for us as a fragrant offering and sacrifice to God*' – that is, the Cross. In other words, love your children as your heavenly Father loves you – with selfless love. Children are not there for us, we are there for them. Unconditional love is that love for a child no matter what he or she looks like, no matter what his or her assets or liabilities are, no matter how they act. This love will not increase or decrease according to their achievements or failures. The message conveyed will be, I love you for who you are and not because of what you have done.

Sadly, it is all too easy to fall into the trap of offering only conditional love. So we have this scenario. A child comes home from school. 'Dad,' he says, 'I came second in the geography exam.' How does Dad reply? 'Good, who came first?' What is the message being sent? It is that Dad will really love me only if I get to the top. And so the vicious treadmill of 'parent pleasing' begins.

But when the child feels they don't succeed, the very resentment which Paul says we should avoid is ignited and becomes very difficult to extinguish.

It is important to recognise that adults are mainly verbally orientated. That is, we often express how we feel by what we say. But children are most behaviourally orientated, actions go a long way with them. And there are three things in particular we need to do day in and day out if our children are going to know deep down they are loved unconditionally.

Love in action

First, there is focused attention. The speaker of CARE for the Family, Rob Parsons, often invites parents to imagine the following scene: It is tea time and the family is gathered around the table. 'Dad, guess what I did at school today?' 'Dad, have you seen what I've drawn?' 'Dad, Billy pushed me over again.' Mum has already heard all of this, she got it the moment they walked in. But, Dad, well, his mind is on something else, it's that same familiar distant look in his eyes – he is there in body but not in spirit. Then the phone rings, it's for him; suddenly, like magic, he is alive, chatting away, giving advice, listening intently to the person on the other end of the phone. His children may not say anything or be able to put it into words but what is firmly lodged in their minds is this thought: 'This is what makes my Dad tick

– not us.' In the United States a survey was conducted amongst young executive fathers to determine how long they spent with their toddler children. First, they ascertained how long they *thought* they spent with them in talking and playing. They replied – about twenty minutes a day. The researchers then fixed them up with microphones and monitored them. The results were shocking. The average time spent with children in meaningful interaction was thirty-seven seconds.

Children need our full, individual attention and that takes time. 'Ah,' we say, 'but I give quality time.' We don't. For we can't choose on our terms when our children will relate to us. It's only as we give quantity time that out of *that* arises quality time – a precious window of opportunity. It is as you are clearing away the toys with your son in his bedroom that he will suddenly say, 'Mum, it's been horrible at school today.' It is as you are sorting out your daughter's cupboard that she will say, 'Dad, someone asked me to go out with him. What should I say?' In our family we have found that washing up together at the sink has provided the most helpful occasions to chat. I can assure you, with rare exceptions will a teenager seek you out for an in-depth talk. However, it is as you are there doing something together that, quite spontaneously, issues will be raised and away you go in conversation. *But* time has to be made.

Linked with focused attention is the importance of eye contact.

It is amazing what we convey with our eyes, often unconsciously – love, anger, approval, disapproval. Have you ever noticed how some people find it difficult to look at you and make eye contact? Their eyes are always darting away. That is a sign of insecurity. But our children need to know they are secure with us and sustained eye contact when we are speaking with them or listening to them conveys the message that they matter. Try it out sometime, look into your children's eyes and note the difference it makes.

Thirdly, there is physical contact. Ross Campbell, in his excellent book *How to Really Love Your Child*, describes how each one of us has an emotional tank which needs filling. Physical touch is vital to that filling – slipping your hand in theirs as you walk together, cuddling up for TV, or sitting on the knee for a bedtime story. You will be amazed at how many children today are undernourished in this biblical sense, suffering from emotional malnutrition – and a television is no substitute. What may surprise many is the knowledge that even when they grow into big, gangly teenagers, they still need their hugs.

No one prepares you for parenthood, do they? No one warns you that your teenage sons will be wearing the same 'T' shirt for six weeks and this will be a familiar sensory experience you have to live with. But at the end of the day, whether they are six months, six years or sixteen – there is one thing required of Christian parents – unconditional love, a mark of the true Spirit-filled life.

Dare to discipline

There is also Christian correction – that is what the word training (*paideia*) means – discipline. This certainly involves punishment, for Paul had not left his Old Testament behind which says. 'He who spares the rod hates his son, but he who loves him is careful to discipline him' (Prov. 13:24).

Without doubt some have used verses like these to justify harsh treatment of children – but that can only be done by ignoring the first part of this verse about not provoking children to resentment and tenderly rearing them. As an over-reaction to this abuse some have gone to the other extreme and would deny any use of physical correction. Again, we must keep the biblical balance. If we have followed through the things we have been looking at in showing unconditional love, then a child will be more ready and able to accept discipline when it has to be given, for he will understand the spirit in which it is given.

Here again are a few pointers.

First, children like to know what are the limits beyond which they cannot go. No limits leads to bewilderment. If you say to a child that they can watch TV for an hour that is clear. If you say they have to be in at a certain time, then you need to stick to it. Of course we need to make changes as appropriate, as circumstances change and children grow older. But what is so frustrating for a child and will inevitably lead to resentment, is if the parent says one thing and then persistently does another. 'Oh, Mum always says that, she won't do anything, neither will Dad.' And where parents are together it is vital that they support each other. There is nothing so demoralising for one parent who says to their child, 'You must not do that,' only to find the other parent coming along and sweeping it all aside or failing to back them up. That is a recipe for friction and failure. If parents disagree about the boundary limits, then it should be sorted out privately and some agreement reached. And one thing is for sure, children will try and play one parent off against another and that has to be resisted.

Second, if a sanction is given, it should be fair and seen through, and certainly not done in rage. The punishment should be proportionate to the offence. I came across someone who as a little girl wanted a doll's house for Christmas and was told that if she woke up on Christmas night it would be taken away. She woke up and the next morning it was gone. That was not fair, and was harsh. Conversely, it is silly making idle threats, though one hears it – 'You do that and you won't have any pocket money for a year.' The children know you don't mean it so why undermine your standing by saying it?

Third, the punishment must not only fit the crime but fit the child. Children vary so much. Some you just have to look at or raise a voice and that is punishment enough. Some will only respond to a well-placed smack, while for others physical punishment is water off a duck's back – something else may be needed to make the point. We need to be wise and flexible.

But, and this is an important but, once the discipline has been carried out that must be the end of it. It must never be extended or the child is persistently reminded of the offence – that will exasperate. Once it is over, then it is focused attention, eye contact, hugs – telling them that is all in the past and you still love them unconditionally.

Christian education

Finally, our children need instruction 'of the Lord'. There are those who say they will leave all spiritual instruction until their children are of an age to make up their own minds. That doesn't work. From a very early age they will already be having their minds formed – they will pick up ideas from school, the home, the TV. Most of those ideas will be anti-Christian. Just think of what parents promise at baptism, that: 'by *their* prayers, example and teaching, the children will learn to be faithful in public worship and private prayer to live by trust in God.' That is crystal clear. That is what we are promising on oath to do. As Christian parents one of our greatest responsibilities, for which we will have to answer to God, is to bring up our children in the Christian faith. Which means, first of all, that we need to grow in the faith ourselves by regularly attending a place of worship week by week with our children and learning together. And, a point which does need underscoring is that fathers are not to leave such instruction to the mothers as if it were their responsibility alone. This exhortation is primarily addressed to fathers. So, fathers, pray with your children, enthuse with them about the Lord Jesus, and show them that Christ makes all the difference in the world.

11

Spiritual Wisdom on Spiritual Warfare
Ephesians 6:10-20

Ephesians 6:10-20

[10]Finally, be strong in the Lord and in his mighty power. [11]Put on the full armour of God so that you can take your stand against the devil's schemes. [12]For our struggle is not against flesh and blood, but against the rulers, against the authorities, against the powers of this dark world and against the spiritual forces of evil in the heavenly realms. [13]Therefore put on the full armour of God, so that when the day of evil comes, you may be able to stand your ground, and after you have done everything, to stand. [14]Stand firm then, with the belt of truth buckled around your waist, with the breastplate of righteousness in place, [15]and with your feet fitted with the readiness that comes from the gospel of peace. [16]In addition to all this, take up the shield of faith, with which you can extinguish all the flaming arrows of the evil one. [17]Take the helmet of salvation and the sword of the Spirit, which is the word of God. [18]And pray in the Spirit on all occasions with all kinds of prayers and requests. With this in mind, be alert and always keep on praying for all the saints.

[19]Pray also for me, that whenever I open my mouth, words may be given me so that I will fearlessly make known the mystery of the gospel, [20]for which I am an ambassador in chains. Pray that I may declare it fearlessly, as I should.

Until the arrival of the blockbuster *Titanic*, George Lucas's Star Wars Trilogy enjoyed the accolade of being the greatest box office hit of all time. Within the Christian circles there is a school of thought which, in its own way, parallels the popularity and ideas of Lucas's cinematic epic, and which we could conveniently call 'Spirit Wars.' Here is one illustrative statement from a recent book which advocates this particular approach to spiritual warfare:

> 'The hypothesis I am suggesting, then, is that ... Satan delegates high ranking members of the hierarchy of evil spirits to control nations, regions, cities, tribes, people, groups, neighbourhoods and other significant social networks of human beings throughout the world. Their major assignment is to prevent God from being glorified in their territory, which they do through directing the activity of low ranking demons.'[1]

That is Peter Wagner in *Wrestling with Angels*. At the more popular level this form of 'spiritual warfare' theory has been promoted by Frank Peretti in his book *This Present Darkness*.

The picture painted is pretty hair-raising stuff and would provide ample material for a Stephen King novel. Put simply, the theory is that what happens in our visible material world, including the power plays of politics, is but a mirroring and

1. Peter Wagner, *Wrestling with Dark Angels*, Regal Books, 1990, p. 77.

outworking of the power plays taking place in the invisible spirit world.

It is argued that the most powerful demons are the territorial spirits who control geographical areas and prevent evangelism from working there. Therefore, for evangelism to go forward the particular demon has first to be identified and his power broken through certain prayer rituals or special marches. I have heard people actually say that the reason why the city of Hull in which I live, is such a spiritually hard place is because of its past associations with witchcraft – the term 'Wyke' for example denoting an area of Hull, is derived from 'Wicca' meaning – witch. When this is combined with the malevolent effect, so it is argued, of the folklore superstitions and practices of seamen, then the city becomes a magnet for evil spirits.

On a personal level this theory postulates that Christians can be demonised. This may be due to a deliberate engagement with occult practices or inadvertently by owning a piece of pagan jewellery. Some would further argue that it is possible for a demon to attach itself to a family line and so be passed down through subsequent generations because a distant relative has been involved in Freemasonry or guilty of a particular sin. One minister relates how his son who attended a well-known Christian college in America was quite depressed. He had been struggling with doubts and had sought out a professor who engages in this modern 'warfare counselling'. The professor asked the young man a few questions and concluded that he certainly was a Christian. He then proceeded to say that a demon of doubt had most likely attached itself to his spirit. The counselling followed this line for some weeks with not so helpful results.

It is therefore not hard to see that if one holds to such views then special 'deliverance ministries' are necessary to combat such forces and to release individuals and, indeed, whole towns from demonic control. The result is that a new priest-hood has emerged – men who are 'in the know', having a special 'anointing' of which ordinary Christians and ministers are ignorant.

If this view of demonic powers is substantially correct, then I for one would not be able to sleep at night and neither should anyone else for that matter! Here we have a fertile breeding ground for all sorts of doubts and anxieties. For invariably it raises questions such as these: could it be that the reason why I find a particular temptation so trying is because my great, great grandfather on my mother's side one day happened to visit a fortune teller on his day out to Blackpool? If so what can I do? By myself very little. I need the deliverance minister. Does that not strike you as remarkably similar to the function of medicine men of pagan religions? Also such deliverance practices are self-generating because if you are told that John is in spiritual difficulty because his auntie used to read the horoscopes, then it might be that the reason you are finding the Christian life a struggle is because of some ancestral skeleton in your cupboard of which you might be totally unaware. The obvious conclusion to draw is that you too need to seek out deliverance. Do you see how it works? What is more, does not this demon-run police state in which Christians are little more than pawns stand in such stark contrast with the light and liberty that the New Testament describes as already theirs who are in Christ? So Paul writes in Ephesians 5:8: 'For you were once darkness, but now you are light in the Lord. Live as children of light.' Nowhere in the New Testament are believers ever depicted as living in servile fear of demons, that is precisely the state from which they have been delivered by the gospel.

The issue, then, is not between those who believe in demons and those who don't. Or between those who believe that Christians are engaged in a spiritual war and those who don't. It is between those who view the spiritual war biblically and those whose view is unbiblical although they may use Scriptural language to promote their ideas. When you consider what the Bible actually teaches about the nature of our spiritual warfare and the means we are to use, you soon discover that it is a million light years away from what many are promoting today.

The classic text Christians turn to in order to gain biblical wisdom on this matter of spiritual warfare is Ephesians 6:10ff.

The location of the spiritual battle

This section about putting on the spiritual armour is not some afterthought that Paul has just tagged on because he had some spare papyrus to fill! It is something he has been building up to throughout this letter. The picture Paul has been painting in the most splendid colours imaginable is of God's eternal plan and purpose for his church which he has put into effect through his Son Jesus Christ. So we read in 3:7-11:

> I became a servant of this gospel by the gift of God's grace given me through the working of his power. Although I am less than the least of all God's people, this grace was given me: to preach to the Gentiles the unsearchable riches of Christ, and to make plain to everyone the administration of this mystery, which for ages past was kept hidden in God, who created all things. His intent was that now, through the church, the manifold wisdom of God should be made known to the rulers and authorities in the heavenly realms, according to his eternal purpose which he accomplished in Christ Jesus our Lord.'

In other words, the church is not only to be the expression of God's wisdom, which is the gospel,

173

but also God's great advertisement of where his plan is heading, viz. 'to gather up all things under one head, even Jesus Christ' (1:10).

We are to notice to whom this surpassing wisdom of God embodied in the church is to be made known, it is to the 'rulers and authorities in the heavenly places' (3:10), that is, the devil and his cohorts which inhabit the invisible spirit world. Since it is the church which is the manifestation of God's plan of redemption and the instrument through which he brings this plan about as the gospel is preached and men and women are saved, doesn't it logically follow that the *main* place where the devil will attack will be in the church itself? It will be the local church, which is an expression of the heavenly church, that the devil will do all in his power to destroy. In other words, the spiritual battlefield will be right amongst the gathering of God's people.

God through the power of the gospel message has achieved in Christian believers the impossible. According to Ephesians 2:1-3, it is men and women outside of Christ who are spiritually 'dead in trespasses and sins' and so under the sway of evil powers. First, in terms of their social and intellectual environment, what is called 'the ways of this world,' that is, thinking and values which are in direct opposition to God – humanism, communism, scientism and all the other 'isms' which treat life as if there is no God. Then there is their own natural inclination towards sin, what is called 'the flesh,' which we are by nature biased against the good. That is why we do not have to teach children to do what is wrong, but we do have to spend a lot of time teaching them to do what is right – 'be kind', 'tell the truth', 'share your toys'. Thirdly, there is the influence of a supernatural opponent, 'the prince of the power of the air' – the devil. It is important to note that Paul does not give priority of one over the other. It is not *all* the devil, we too are responsible for our sin, the choices we make, the ideologies we promote. Certainly, the devil may egg us on, but let us not give him all the credit.

But, says Paul, by the gospel Christians are placed into an entirely different position. They are now part of a supernatural body, the church, in which God dwells by his Spirit (2:22). Christians are no longer slaves to evil forces on the wrong side of God, but 'through faith in Christ can approach God with freedom and confidence' (3:12). As Christians belonging to the family of the church we are 'to be strong in the Lord and in his mighty power' (6:10), all made available to us by Christ's victory on the cross once and for all (1:7).

Certainly, Christians will still be tempted to do wrong, for they still have a body poisoned by sin. They will still be tempted to run after the world and adopt its fashions, even within the church – health and wealth, name it and claim it teaching, partying for Christ instead of proclaiming Christ. They will still be the objects of Satan's attacks, perhaps more so now, at least with a greater degree of awareness.

The nature of the warfare

If the main focus of the spiritual battle centres on the church what is the nature of this battle?

Paul writes in 6:12: 'For our struggle is not against flesh and blood, but against the rulers, against the authorities, against the powers of this dark world and against the spiritual forces of evil in the heavenly realms.' The word translated 'struggle' is *pale,* a word found nowhere else in the Greek New Testament. But it is found a lot in the contemporary Graeco-Roman world, although not in the world of warfare, but in the world of *wrestling.* Paul is teaching that the church is involved in a hand to hand struggle. It is a spiritual struggle against spiritual forces. However, before we get carried away thinking that we are back into some spirit wars of the Frank Perriti type, it is vital that we look at what Paul says earlier about the way the devil works in the church. And it sounds so familiar.

In 6:11 he talks about the devil's 'schemes', literally, stratagems. That is a phrase which appears in 4:14, where Paul writes concerning the need for Christians to grow in biblical knowledge so that they might not be 'blown here and there by every wind of teaching and by the cunning and craftiness of men and their deceitful *stratagems*'. In other words, the devil will try and destroy the church from within by false teaching, including the false teaching that Christians can be demonised and need deliverance ministry! That is the type of belief that will lead Christians back into a form of slavish dependence and fear. The bitter irony is that for all their talk of the devil, those who would scare Christians into under-valuing the power of the gospel and the liberty they have in the Lord Jesus, are doing the devil's work for him.

Where else is the devil mentioned in Ephesians? In 4:27: 'Do not give the devil a foothold.' How? Well, that injunction comes in the middle of some very practical teaching about the way Christians are meant to behave in the body of Christ because of their new life in Christ (vv.25-32):

> Therefore each of you must put off falsehood and speak truthfully to his neighbor, for we are all members of one body. [26]'In your anger do not sin': Do not let the sun go down while you are still angry, [27]and do not give the devil a foothold. [28]He who has been stealing must steal no longer, but must work, doing something useful with his own hands, that he may have something to share with those in need.
>
> [29]Do not let any unwholesome talk come out of

your mouths, but only what is helpful for building others up according to their needs, that it may benefit those who listen. [30]And do not grieve the Holy Spirit of God, with whom you were sealed for the day of redemption. [31]Get rid of all bitterness, rage and anger, brawling and slander, along with every form of malice. [32]Be kind and compassionate to one another, forgiving each other, just as in Christ God forgave you.

This means the devil will try to destroy us by leading us into immoral behaviour. That is a real struggle for every Christian. Which is easier: to march around the city and claim it for Christ or to stop running down a fellow believer behind her back? Which is the more demanding: to pray over someone that the demon of jealousy be cast out or going up to someone and asking their forgiveness for the way you have hurt them by your cutting remarks inspired by your jealousy? I know which is a real wrestling match for me. This is where the real battle lies in Christian relationships, putting into practice at personal cost Christian truth – not some imaginary Dungeon and Dragons world.

The means of fighting the battle

What, then, are the means by which we are to conduct this spiritual war? Paul tells us: by collectively putting on *God's* armour – an allusion to Isaiah 59:17: 'He put on righteousness as his breastplate, and the helmet of salvation on his head; he put on the garments of vengeance and wrapped himself in zeal as in a cloak.'

It is important that we do not let the armour metaphor mesmerise us into drawing us off in the wrong direction. It is there to remind us we are in a fight, that the fight is God's and it will ultimately be victorious. But when we put the metaphorical language to one side and concentrate on the substance of what Paul is teaching it seems so mundane, almost banal.

Paul speaks of the necessity of truth (v.14). Paul has already been talking in 4:15 concerning the importance of true doctrine over and against false doctrine as well as the absolute necessity of speaking truthfully to each other rather than deceiving.

Then there is evangelism – a sure way to get the devil on the run – that is what he means by the phrase the 'gospel of peace' in verse 15. That is how the church in Ephesus was established in the first place. In the account of Luke in Acts 19, we do not find Paul organising a march or calling a special prayer meeting to overthrow the territorial spirits located in the temple of Diana. In fact he did something really revolutionary — and more demanding; he preached the gospel! He went to the synagogue and argued. After he was thrown out of there he hired a hall for a series of lunchtime lectures over a period of two years. Through this 'in depth' evangelism people were actually converted and when they came to a saving knowledge of Christ *then* they burnt all their magic books. Note that there was no special ritual for those involved in the occult, just hearing and believing the gospel. That doesn't mean Paul did not pray, for in 6:19 he asks for prayer so that he would be fearless in evangelism – not praying for the power of territorial spirits to be broken. Paul knew the devil to be more subtle than that – making us scared of telling others or distracting us into other ministries instead of the ministry of the Word.

We are also called to exercise trust in God (v.16), not in techniques. In addition we are to take hold of the full salvation we have in Christ and understand our status before God – the righteousness he gives us (v.17). All of these things relate to the gospel which is God's truth, in which we are to have faith, through which we are saved and made righteous. And where do we find the gospel but in the Word of God, which is the sword of the Spirit. So it is vital that we study it and teach it.

Finally, all of these things are to be joined together by prayer: 'Pray in the Spirit on all occasions for all the saints' (v.18). What other kind of praying is there but prayer in the Spirit? Of course all of this is very hard work, why else is the prayer meeting the worst attended meeting in any church? For that is where the battle is.

The objective of the spiritual battle

What is the goal of this warfare? To disarm angelic beings? No! Christ has already done that on the cross, as we read in Colossians 2:15: 'And having disarmed the powers and authorities, he made a public spectacle of them, triumphing over them by the cross.' It is simply that we take a stand, remain immovable, and that paradoxically is to advance. You advance by standing firm – as Paul repeats in Ephesians 6:11, 13 and 14. Can you imagine the effect of a church in which prayer for each other is constant and loving, in which the truth is taught faithfully and accepted believingly? Think of the impression that would make upon the cities of our land as the gospel is proclaimed and Jesus Christ is enthroned in the hearts of men and women.

There is no new ministry or means of spiritual warfare. We are called to keep on with what Christians have always been called on to do – believe, proclaim, pray and live the gospel. This is wisdom to live by, the wisdom of the gospel of Christ who is 'our wisdom'.

Melvin Tinker is Vicar of St. John's Newland in Hull. He read theology at Oxford and trained for ordination at Wycliffe Hall, before becoming a curate at Wetherby Parish Church in Yorkshire. Prior to his current position he was Anglican Chaplain to the University of Keele in Staffordshire. He has written on a wide variety of subjects relating to doctrine and ethics and was the editor of *Restoring the Vision - 'Anglicans Speak Out'* (Monarch, 1990) and *The Anglican Evangelical Crisis!* (Christian Focus Publications, 1995). He is married to Heather and they have three boys.

Christian Focus publishes two other titles by Melvin Tinker. One is called *Why Do Bad Things Happen to Good People* and considers what the Bible has to say about the problem of suffering. His other book is *Close Encounters* which examines conversations several people had with Jesus (as recorded in the Gospel of John). A chapter from this book is included in the following pages.

1

Jesus meets a doubter
(John 20:24-31)

Let me give ten reasons why I don't wash:

1. I was made to wash as a child and that put me off.
2. People who wash are hypocrites, everyone knows that, for they reckon they are cleaner than other people.
3. There are so many different kinds of soap, I couldn't possibly decide how to choose between them.
4. I used to wash, but it got rather boring so I gave it up.
5. I only wash on special occasions, like Easter and Christmas.
6. I'm still young. When I get older and a little dirtier I might turn to washing then.
7. I really don't have time, I am far too busy to wash.
8. None of my other friends wash, so why should I?
9. The bathroom's never warm enough.
10. People who make soap are only after your money.

You will have noticed that this list is remarkably similar to the standard objections to Christianity and church attendance, which, when put like that, highlight how unreasonable they are. But what about this for an objection?: 'What I can't stand about Christians is that they are so gullible. It's all a matter of faith. As for me, I'm a down-to-earth sort of person, hard nosed. I deal with facts not faith – give me some proof.' Is the objector right? Is faith somehow opposed to facts and therefore more like fantasy, believing six impossible things before breakfast?

The story we are looking at in this chapter demonstrates once and for all that it is not a matter of having to choose between faith and facts, but that true faith is based upon facts. This is brought out in this amazing story of the encounter between the disciple Thomas and the risen Lord Jesus in John 20.

That I can't believe

Now Thomas (called Didymus), one of the Twelve, was not with the disciples when Jesus came ... the other disciples told him that they had seen the Lord (20:24-25).

This was the setting: Jesus had been brutally executed. Consequently the disciples were huddled behind locked doors, hiding in fear lest the Roman authorities do to them what they did to their Master. Suddenly, Jesus appeared out of nowhere. There he was in flesh and blood standing before them. Admittedly it was a transformed body, but a corporeal body nonetheless.

So you can imagine the enthusiasm with which the disciples would have told Thomas the wonderful news that Jesus was the Messiah after all, that death could not hold him.

But how did Thomas reply? 'Marvellous news, just what I've been waiting to hear'? On the contrary: *'Unless I see the nail marks in his hands and put my finger where the nails were, and put my hand into his side, I will not believe it'* (20:25).

That's a stringent demand that Thomas is making, one which would have made any logical positivist proud: 'I don't only want to see him, I want to touch him. And not only do I want to touch him, I want irrefutable proof that he really is the one I saw crucified and not some impostor, and that means feeling the holes in his hands, and inserting my hand into his side which was lacerated by a spear. If

184

I can't do that I won't believe.' Not I can't believe, but I *won't* believe.

Is there not a note of defiance here? Is not Thomas laying down demands which are plainly unreasonable? It certainly seems that way. It is all very much in line with what Jesus constantly encountered throughout his ministry and which Paul targets in 1 Corinthians 1, namely, that the 'Jews *demand* signs'. In fact, this became a barrier to belief.

The same principle operates today. We say: I will devote myself to God *if* he heals my child. I will follow Jesus *if* he mends my marriage. I will happily become a Christian *if* God proves himself to me in a tangible way, performing a miracle on demand. In each of these cases, it is not God who is called to assess us, but we who are assessing him, demanding that he jump through the hoops we set up.

In effect we are laying down the conditions God must meet if he is to have the privilege of our company. But not only is this the height of arrogance, it is the height of folly. For what if Christianity is true and God refuses (as is his right) to meet our preconditions? Then we forfeit knowing him for ever. What if God has given us plenty of reasons for belief, evidences for trusting him (which, as we shall see in a moment, he has), and yet by sticking to our prior demands we ignore them? Then we are as foolish as the man who loses his wife because he has laid down that unless she cooks him perfect eggs for breakfast each morning she can't really love him. The wrong criteria have been employed.

Seeing is believing?
Whether Thomas was really expecting his demands to be met we can't be sure, but one thing is for certain, he was

185

in for a very big surprise: *A week later his disciples were in the house again, and Thomas was with them. Though the doors were locked, Jesus came and stood among them and said, 'Peace be with you.' Then he said to Thomas, 'Put your finger here; see my hands. Reach out your hand and put it into my side. Stop doubting and believe'* (20:26-27).

How incredibly kind of Jesus! He could have let Thomas stew in his own unbelieving juice. Instead, in a remarkable act of loving condescension, the risen Jesus appears with the specific intention of addressing Thomas. Wonderfully, the first words Jesus utters are words of comfort: 'Peace be with you.'

This is not some pious greeting akin to a sanctimonious 'Bless you', nor the first-century equivalent to our 'Have a nice day'. Here we have the crucified and risen Lord of all creation giving words of deep reassurance, the assurance that there is now peace with God. Through his work on the cross, dying as a sacrifice for sins in the place of rebels like us, he has now cleared the way back to God whereby we can approach him as children of a heavenly Father. Given what Thomas had just done, not only in deserting Jesus with the rest of the disciples, but in exercising sinful unbelief, those were precisely the words he needed to hear most of all.

But in addition to words of reassurance, Jesus issued words of rebuke. 'Alright Thomas, have it your way if you must. Put your finger in my side which was torn for you, touch the nail-scarred hands that were pierced for you. Stop disbelieving and show yourself a believer.' That is the way the original can be translated: 'cease disbelieving and believe'.

Some have taken these verses as a justification for the church to allow doubters into the ranks of its leaders.

Thomas doubted, he was a leader, yet he was accepted by Jesus. Thus, they say, we are obliged to do the same; doubting bishops are legitimate. But clearly that was not Jesus' intention. This stands as a ticking off for Thomas, not a commendation of how God loves the critical doubter!

Thomas was being told to stop acting like an unbeliever and instead show himself as a true believer. It is not enough simply to believe in God. Thomas did that, he was a good Jew. It is not enough to be associated with Jesus. Thomas had been with Jesus through thick and thin for nearly three years. Nor is it enough to be with those who follow Jesus. Thomas was at least gathered with the other disciples. Something more is required, and just what that something is can be seen in those immortal words that Thomas uttered, *'My Lord and my God'* (20:28).

Thomas was not being profane at this point. This was not the unthinking reaction of a startled man. This is nothing less than a deep personal profession of faith which must be made by anyone who wishes to become a true Christian. This is not blind faith, for the evidence is now too overwhelming, so much so that Thomas did not even bother with his original demands of touching Jesus. Nor is it some vague belief in the divine Other. Rather, this is believing faith which has Jesus as its object. There are two things about this faith which we need to take to heart.

First, this belief is *confessional*. It involves believing a truth. Who is Jesus? He is Lord and God, that's who. This is an amazing confession when you consider the context. The claim is being made that embodied in this crucified carpenter is none other than the Creator of the universe – he is God. Standing before Thomas in magisterial power is the one who demands our submission

187

to his rule for *de facto* he is the ruler of the world, he is Lord.

But this was not mere head knowledge for Thomas, the equivalent to the Apostles Creed which can so easily roll off the tongue, parrot fashion, without engaging the heart or mind. It is a *personal profession of faith*, hence the possessive pronoun, '*My* Lord and *my* God'.

In other words, what lies at the heart of the Christian faith is not religion as such, but a relationship. There are plenty of people in churches up and down the country who are steeped in religion, going through the motions of church attendance, but who have not the faintest idea of what it means to have a personal relationship with God, simply because they have never come to that point where they have submitted to Jesus as *their* ruler and redeemer.

In the middle of the last century, there was a Vicar in Cornwall by the name of William Haslam.[1] One day, much to his surprise, his gardener became a Christian and he didn't quite know what to make of this. He visited a friend who told him bluntly that the reason why he didn't understand was because he himself was not yet converted.

His friend asked him: 'Have you peace with God?'

To which Haslam replied, 'Of course, God is my friend.'

Pursuing the point further, his colleague asked him, 'How did you get that peace?'

'Oh,' replied the Vicar, 'I get it at the daily service. I get it through prayer and reading and especially at Holy Communion. I have made it a rule to carry my sins there every Sunday, and often come away from the holy Sacrament feeling happy and as free as a bird.'

'And how long does this peace last?' enquired his friend.

'I suppose not a week,' said Haslam thoughtfully, 'for

I have to do the same thing every Sunday.'

The friend then went on to tell him about the living waters that Jesus promised, welling up from within to eternal life. William Haslam then admitted that he did not know of such a thing, but would dearly love to have it. Then he left.

The following Sunday, Haslam climbed into his pulpit and announced the text, 'What think ye of Christ?' This is how he describes what happened next.

'As I went on to explain the passage, I saw that the Pharisees and Scribes did not know that Christ was the Son of God or that he came to save them. Something was telling me all the time, "You are no better than the Pharisees yourself, you do not believe he is the Son of God and that he came to save you any more than they did."

'I do not remember all I said, but I felt a wonderful light and joy coming into my soul, and I was beginning to see what the Pharisees did not. Whether it was my words or my manner or my look, I know not; but all of a sudden a local preacher, who happened to be in the congregation, stood up and putting up his arms shouted out in a Cornish manner, "The parson is converted! the parson is converted! Hallelujah." And in another moment his voice was lost in the shouts and praises of three or four hundred in the congregation. Instead of rebuking this extraordinary brawling as I would have done at one time, I joined in the outburst of praise.'

He then describes how at least twenty people in the congregation cried out for mercy and professed to find joy and peace in believing, including three members of Haslam's own family. The news spread like wildfire throughout the town that the Vicar had been converted by his own sermon!

Like Haslam and Thomas, it is only too possible to be an acquaintance of Christ and yet not a full-blooded believer in Christ. Many a person has a religious standing and yet knows nothing of the forgiveness and peace Christ alone can bring.

The question raised by this incident is: Have you, like Thomas, come to the point where you have personally come before Christ in heartfelt sorrow and trust saying, 'My Lord and my God'? If not, then whatever you may wish to call yourself, you are not yet a Christian.

Believing is seeing

But you may object saying, 'It was alright for Thomas, he saw Jesus face to face. I would believe if confronted with irrefutable proof like that.' Really? Jesus views the matter differently. *Then Jesus told him, 'Because you have seen me, you have believed, blessed are those who have not seen and yet have believed'* (20:29).

I do not have to travel in a space shuttle and look down upon the world to believe that it is round. Others have done that and I have sufficient reason to trust their testimony. Neither do I have to see Jesus bodily to believe that he has been raised from the dead. Others have seen him and I trust their reports with good cause.[2] All the evidence we need to convince any fair-minded person beyond any reasonable doubt that Jesus is God who became man is to be found in the Bible.

Today, claims are being made in some quarters that we need signs and wonders, special miracles to be performed as part of our evangelism, in order to convince a sceptical generation about the truth of Christianity. John would place a serious question mark against such claims.

As far as he is concerned all the signs and wonders we need are contained in his Gospel. He doesn't say, 'By the way, after reading this you may want some confirmatory proof, so why don't you search out your nearest Christian gathering and ask them to perform a few miracles for you.' Far from it. He writes: *These are written* (including reliable accounts of miracles performed by Jesus) *that you may believe that Jesus is the Christ, and that by believing you may have life in his name* (20:31), that is, genuine spiritual life.

If you think that this is not enough, all I can say is that you are claiming that God and John are mistaken, for they think what has been given is sufficient. Admittedly, the evidence is not exhaustive (John says so himself in verse 25 of the next chapter: *Jesus did many other things as well. If every one of them were written down, I suppose that even the whole world would not have room for the books that would be written*). However, the evidence is substantial and sufficient.

God never asks us to exercise blind faith in becoming a follower of Christ, but he does call us to have an open faith, a reasonable trust in his dear Son, based upon the evidence he has so kindly given in his respect for our integrity. Is such a trust too much to ask for? 'Stop unbelieving and show yourself a believer,' says Jesus to Thomas, and to us.

References
1. Revd W. Haslam, *From Death Unto Life*, Good News Crusade, St Austell, Cornwall, 1979
2. For example, see George E. Ladd, *I Believe in the Resurrection*, Hodder and Stoughton, 1975.

Christian Focus Publications publishes biblically-accurate books for adults and children. The books in the adult range are published in three imprints.

Christian Heritage contains classic writings from the past.

Christian Focus contains popular works including biographies, commentaries, doctrine, and Christian living.

Mentor focuses on books written at a level suitable for Bible College and seminary students, pastors, and others; the imprint includes commentaries, doctrinal studies, examination of current issues, and church history.

For a free catalogue of all our titles, please write to
Christian Focus Publications,
Geanies House, Fearn,
Ross-shire, IV20 1TW, Great Britain

For details of our titles visit us on our web site
http://www.christianfocus.com